Hypertext Handbook

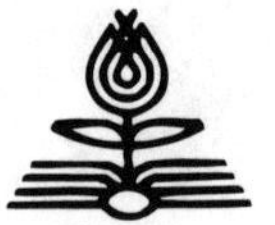

PETER LANG
New York • Washington, D.C./Baltimore • Bern
Frankfurt am Main • Berlin • Brussels • Vienna • Oxford

Andreas Kitzmann

Hypertext Handbook

The Straight Story

PETER LANG
New York • Washington, D.C./Baltimore • Bern
Frankfurt am Main • Berlin • Brussels • Vienna • Oxford

Library of Congress Cataloging-in-Publication Data

Kitzmann, Andreas.
Hypertext handbook: the straight story / Andreas Kitzmann.
p. cm.
Includes bibliographical references and index.
1. Hypertext systems. 2. Literature and technology.
3. Mass media—Philosophy. I. Title.
QA76.76.H94K478 006.7—dc22 2006019388
ISBN 0-8204-7441-X

Bibliographic information published by **Die Deutsche Bibliothek**.
Die Deutsche Bibliothek lists this publication in the "Deutsche Nationalbibliografie"; detailed bibliographic data is available on the Internet at http://dnb.ddb.de/.

Cover art credit: Rafael Lozano-Hemmer, "Under Scan,"
a large scale public art project featuring 1,000 interactive portraits.
Commissioned by the East Midlands Development Agency, UK 2006

Cover design by Lisa Barfield

The paper in this book meets the guidelines for permanence and durability of the Committee on Production Guidelines for Book Longevity of the Council of Library Resources.

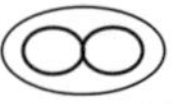

29 Broadway, New York, NY 10006
www.peterlang.com

Printed in the United States of America

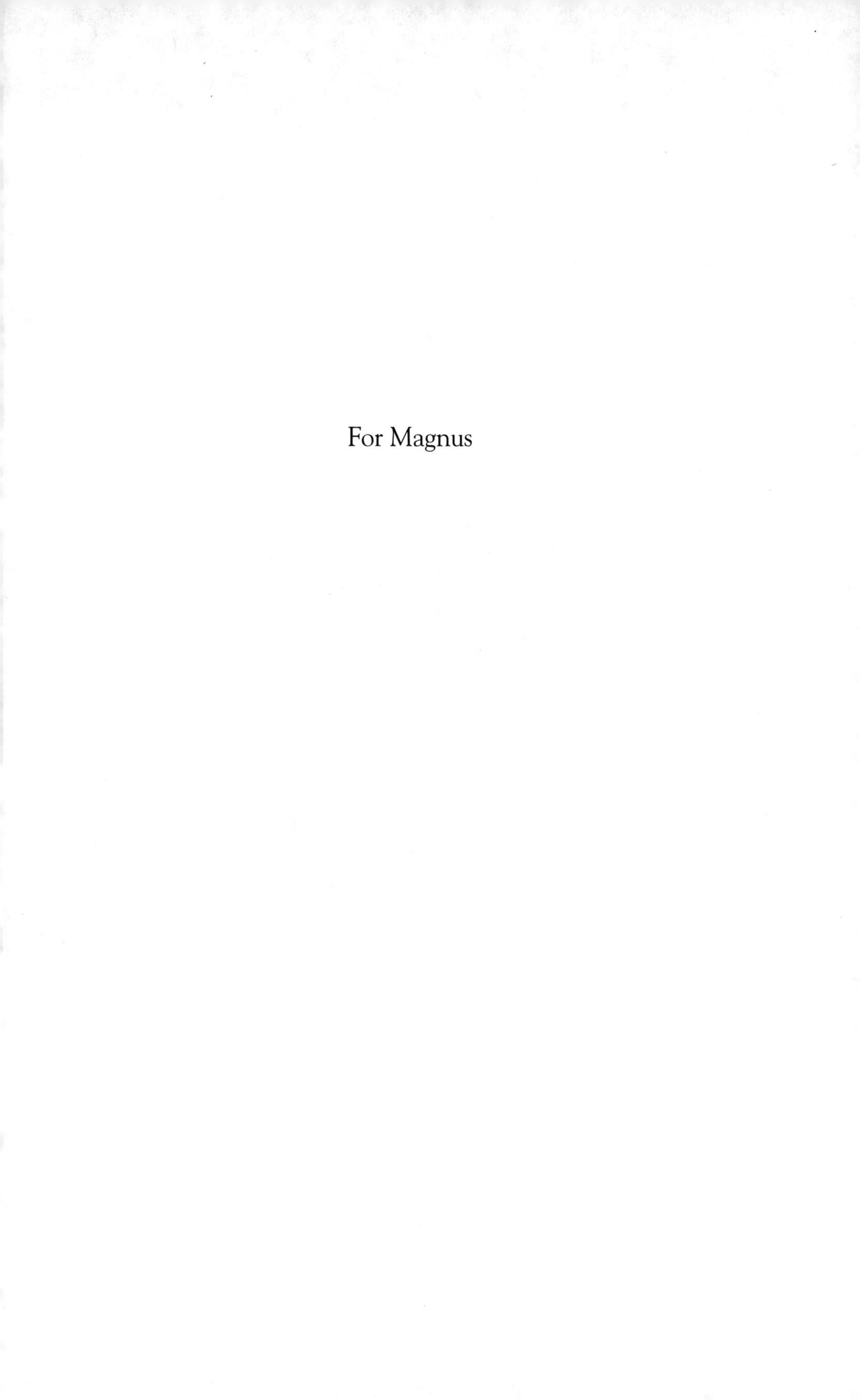

For Magnus

Contents

Preface

I first discovered hypertext in the summer of 1992 when I happened upon Robert Coover's canonical article "The End of Books" published in the *New York Times Book Review*. At that time I was struggling with the topic of my doctoral dissertation, which, as I recall had something to do with Franz Kafka and identity. After reading Coover's article I realized that I had to switch topics and quickly fired off a hastily constructed proposal to my ever-tolerant adviser. A few years later and after the usual turmoil that comes with the territory of graduate studies, I managed to successfully write and defend my dissertation, which has the rather unwieldy title "The Melancholic Hypertext: The Fate of the Writer in the Tangential Narrative."

Since then hypertext has come in and out of my life both in terms of research and teaching. In general, my experiences with the early hyperfictions created during what Coover has dubbed the "golden age of hypertext" has lead me to explore and appreciate the extent to which digital media has challenged and reconfigured the manner in which we represent ourselves and our world to one another. Some of these challenges and reconfigurations have yielded impressive results. Others, however, have faded away into the realm of forgotten ideas.

This book is a natural outcome of my previous academic work in hypertext and, as well, incorporates insights and experiences related to my attempts to explain hypertext to sometimes interested and occasionally baffled students. Throughout the years I have benefited from the insights of writers, scholars, students and artists too numerous to mention. I have also benefited from the support of my colleagues at the School of Arts and Letters at York University. Thanks must also go to Damon Zucca at Peter Lang for initially encouraging me to take on this project and his continued and enthusiastic support and advice. Finally, thanks must go to my family and to my new son Magnus who has given nonlinearity an entirely new meaning and realm of experience (for me, at least).

Acknowledgements

The author gratefully thanks the following companies, authors and artists who have given permission to reproduce their work.

Mark Amerika (in collaboration with John Vega and Chad Mossholder) for the screenshots from *Filmtext 2.0* (2001–2002) <www.markamerika.com/filmtext>

Mark Bernstein of Eastgate Systems for the screenshot of a Storyspace map view and the screenshots from Carolyn Guyer's *Quibbling* (Eastgate Systems, 1992).

Natalie Bookchin for the screenshot from *The Intruder*. <http://www.calarts.edu/~bookchin/intruder/>

Linda Carroli and Josephine Wilson for the screenshot from Water Writes Always in Plural. <http://ensemble.va.com.au/water/>

Carolyn Guyer for the screenshots from Quibbling (Eastgate Systems, 1992).

Jörg Haake and Weigang Wang for the screenshot of the CHIPS voting system. Reproduced with permission from *Information and Software Technology*, 41 (1999).

Mable Kinzie for the screenshot of *Net Frog: Digital Dissections*, copyright 1994 & 2002. <http://www.teach.virginia.edu/go/frog>

Rafael Lozano-Hemmer for the image from "Under Scan: Relational Architecture 11.

Judy Malloy for the screenshot from *Revelations of Secret Surveillance*. Copyright 2004. <http://www.well.com/user/jmalloy/gunterandgwen/titlepage.html>

Dane Watkins for the screenshot from HIM. <http://www.eastgate.com/ReadingRoom.html>

Introduction

In many ways, hypertext is a confounding topic. For the most part the concept is simple enough. Theodor Nelson, who coined the term over thirty years ago, defined it simply as "nonsequential writing—text that branches and allows choice to the reader, best read at an interactive screen. As popularly conceived, this is a series of text chunks connected by links which offer the reader different pathways."[1] Nelson's definition sounds remarkably like the current manifestation of the World Wide Web and, as such, is a familiar and normative experience for millions of people around the world. In other words, hypertext is part of everyday life and in that respect would seem to require no further explanation. Therefore, this book, which aims to define and explain hypertext, could end right here.

Yet, despite such apparent simplicity, hypertext verges on being indescribable, at least if one wishes to capture the potential of this complex medium. Indeed, when it comes to pursuing the intricacies of hypertext, especially in terms of its application in more creative endeavors, such as literature, art and poetry, the language deployed often takes a quick turn into the ephemeral. Consider, for example, this definition by the philosophers Mark Taylor and Esa Saarinen:

> A hypertext is not a closed work but an open fabric of heterogeneous traces and associations that are in a process of constant revision and supplementation. The structure of a hypertext is not fixed but is forever shifting and always mobile. ... Everything everywhere is middle. Instead of an organic whole, a hypertext is a rent texture whose meaning is unstable and whose boundaries are constantly changing.[2]

Taylor's and Saarinen's definition is certainly evocative and does a good job of describing the experience or "feeling" of hypertext. As well, it also captures some of the complexities that lurk behind the apparent utility of hypertext as a reading/writing technology. For what is significant about hypertext, at least from the perspective of scholars such as Taylor and Saarinen, is its potential to radically challenge the conventions and practices of literate culture and by extension the conventions of self-expression and knowledge. Hypertext is thus more than just a new tool. It is, to quote Ted Nelson again, a veritable "dream machine" that has the potential to radically alter the way in which we see and understand our world.

It is around such claims or concepts of the ability of hypertext to radically change modes of writing, reading and thinking that the scholarship on hypertext becomes in itself hypertextual in the sense of weaving between multiple references and incorporating the "nonlinear" aesthetic of postmodern writing and critical theory. And it is at this juncture that many newcomers to hypertext become "lost in the maze," to use a favorite hypertext metaphor. What once appeared straightforward and normative quickly becomes shrouded in a labyrinth of complex word play, intertextuality and an ever-expanding list of neologisms.

> One particular meaning of network in relation to hypertext comes close to matching the use of the term in critical theory. Network in this fullest sense refers to the entirety of all those terms for which there is no term and for which other terms stand until something better comes along, or until one of them gathers fuller meanings and fuller acceptance to itself: "literature," "infoworld," "docuverse," in fact "all writing" in the alphanumeric as well as Derridean senses.[3]

The aim of this book is to, as the title suggests, provide a condensed and straightforward introduction to the main issues, concepts and developments of what I would like to call "expressive hypertext" and its interpretation by the academic community. Expressive hypertext is a rough umbrella term that indicates uses of the medium for purposes of expressing ideas, concepts and thoughts as opposed to uses that are purely utilitarian such as in the case of interactive databases. Accordingly, the examples discussed in this volume will privilege uses that are primarily "expressive," whether in the context of literature, art or personal expression and communication. Although it is admittedly difficult to neatly identify the point at which pure information gives way to expression (as in the case of database art), the distinction of expressive hypertext at the very least focuses our attention on issues directly related to how technology affects our habits of representation and communication. In addition, this book will also provide a condensed and selective history of the general medium of hypertext in an effort to engender a context with which to better understand contemporary directions and implications. This latter aim is important for addressing questions that I have often been asked within the classroom: Why does all this stuff about hypertext matter? Why is it necessary to go on and on about how complex hypertext is? Isn't it enough to just understand the basic idea and move on? Such questions are not limited to my own experiences as a teacher. Rather they indicate the need to ground discussions of hypertext within the larger context of the intertwined histories of digital technology and media. In other words, hypertext (as both an application and an arena for academic and artistic inquiry) serves as a valuable case study to better understand how developments in media technology affect not only practice (i.e., what we do with the technology) but also the discourses and paradigms constructed around it. Furthermore, both the discursive and the material manifestations of hypertext provide insight into how technology in general shapes and informs our "lifeworld" in a manner that is essentially codeterminous. Thus, technology becomes more than just a receptacle of culture or a "metaphor" with which to articulate specific concepts or ideas *about* technology. It is a veritable agent that can "act" in ways that cannot be entirely accounted for or predicted via the cultural circumstances that surround it.

But to be clear and thus keep to my aim of providing the "straight story" of hypertext, I will rephrase the above discussion as follows:

1. Hypertext is a technological application that allows readers or viewers to access content in various orders. It is thus a collection of links rather than a single body of linear information or content.
2. Literary hypertext has generated not only an interesting and at times a confounding body of work but also a multitude of academic writing that theorizes the complex implications of hypertext on reading, writing and thinking.
3. This body of work and writing tells us not only about hypertext but also about the manner in which media technology affects the way in which we see and understand our world.
4. Hypertext serves as a valuable case study to better understand the nature of technology and its involvement in what we know and understand as reality.

Also to be addressed is the observation that hypertext is essentially "old news," and that many of the claims made during the late 1980s and early 1990s have failed to materialize in any significant form. Yet, such an apparent "failure" on the part of hypertext should not be taken as a sign that the technology or its associated theories are irrelevant or outdated. On the contrary, the story of hypertext, including its "failure," provides an opportunity to situate it within the broader terrain of contemporary media practice as well as to probe how its development and theorization have been informed and prompted by specific historical and ideological contexts.

It is in this respect that hypertext (as a practice and as an academic subject) again functions as a historical case study that can be used to broaden our understanding of digital media and its impact on cultural production and self-expression.

Major Themes

This book is organized around a sequence of four compact chapters that each deals with a set of limited concerns. Before outlining these chapters, however, I would like to formalize a distinction that will serve as a type of guiding paradigm for the remainder of this volume. This distinction is between two basic modes by which hypertext can be approached. The first is what could be termed the "material mode," which is indicative of the practical or physical ways in which hypertext technology has been developed, implemented and adapted by individuals and institutions. In other words, what is of interest here is basically what people do with hypertext and, by extension, the various realizations or forms of hypertext that are currently available to us. The second mode can be termed as "discursive." Here the main concern is with how hypertext has been talked about, to put it simply. More specifically, the discursive mode draws attention to the various ways in which hypertext has been discursively constructed—the history of hypertext, the claims and predictions about hypertext, the "myths" of hypertext, the theorization of hypertext, the making of hypertext into an academic subdiscipline and so on. What all these discursive areas represent, in short, are particular "stories" or statements regarding the impact and significance of hypertext. These stories are an important part of the overall history of the medium and also provide a means with which to clarify why hypertext still matters.

The discursive mode of hypertext is at the forefront of this book's first chapter and provides a brief history of hypertext in terms of its origins and general development within technical, academic and literary/artistic circles. In addition to providing details regarding major figures and developmental stages, the chapter also draws attention to how the history of hypertext has been formed into an identifiable narrative in terms of expressing particular themes, assumptions and ideologies with respect to technology's role in the continued evolution of the human species. Instrumental here is the concept of progress and a general commitment to what Jody Berland has aptly identified as "technological evolutionism," by which "digital technologies propel our evolution into a postnational, postspatial, postembodied, perhaps posthuman community."[4] It is in this regard that the claims regarding hypertext's radical potential to upset the status quo are effectively compromised. The story of hypertext is very much a normative or mainstream story of progress via the rational application of technology and scientific management and, as such, is less of an alternative to conventional cultural, economic and technological conditions than much of the literature would lead one to believe.

The second chapter focuses on material concerns in terms of identifying common hypertext practices. The basic aim here is to provide concrete and practical examples of how hypertext has been used by a range of engineers, academics, writers, artists and general enthusiasts. Such a mapping of common uses and normative practices is useful for gaining a broad understanding of the major conventions, genres and future directions of hypertext. This will provide a platform to pursue more detailed work on the medium and gain an informed appreciation of hypertext's unique and potentially transformative characteristics. Among the examples to be examined are the literary and artistic uses of hypertext, such as the various attempts at hyperfiction; the educational uses of hypertext technology, especially as a tool for developing writing skills; the uses of hypertext within the work environment and the uses of hypertext within the broad context of computer gaming.

The third chapter returns to the discursive mode by focusing on the manner in which literary hypertext, in particular, has served as a platform from which to engage in a wide variety of theoretical investigations, particularly in terms of questioning the relationship between writers, readers and the material "object" of the text, such as a book or computer screen. Indeed, for many scholars hypertext has been heralded as the medium that provides a concrete realization of the major concepts associated with contemporary critical and literary theory, especially post-structuralism and postmodernism. It is here that the discussion of literary hypertext begins to become difficult and increasingly prone to speculative and at times overwrought theorization. The aim of this chapter is to outline, as clearly as possible, the major theoretical concepts that have been associated with literary hypertext and, more importantly, to identify how such concepts are useful for both understanding and working with the medium itself. Accordingly, the emphasis here is on broadening the understanding and appreciation of hypertext itself, rather than on employing selected readings of individual hypertexts to shore up particular theoretical positions.

The final chapter deals with a merger of both the material and discursive modes of hypertext by focusing on and critiquing what we might call the "hype" of hypertext. Often heralded as a veritable freedom machine, hypertext has been described as a powerful tool for preserving democracy, self-expression and creative thinking. Despite such predictions and the rise of a small but dedicated "hypertext industry" in the early- to mid-1990s hypertext has not actually created the revolutions predicted by the likes of Theodor Nelson and Robert Coover. The conventional book, with its linear and sedentary pages, is still the major vehicle for literary expression, and popular uses of hypertext are generally limited to surfing the World Wide Web or scrolling through the menus of Microsoft Word. Accordingly, this book will conclude by considering the future of hypertext, especially in comparison with the claims and prophesies made by various scholars and visionaries. As mentioned above, I will also use hypertext as a historical case study in order to rethink the nature and role of interactive media within the broader context of contemporary media practice. Among the conclusions is the assertion that hypertext's exploration of interactivity, nonlinearity and participatory media have been limited by the overreliance on literary theory and narrative media. Though understandable in terms of its historical context, the time has now come to continue the exploration of hypertext via theoretical paradigms that draw from a wider sphere of influence and, moreover, that take into account the more recent developments within digital media as a whole, particularly games, the World Wide Web and interactive art and entertainment. That said, hypertext offers an important theoretical legacy with which to further pursue the intriguing possibilities of interactive digital media. This book hopes to make that message clear by delivering the "straight goods" regarding hypertext's important position in the ongoing saga of digital culture.

chapter 1

A Brief History of Hypertext: Origins and Influences

As with any historical account, the history of hypertext is more than just a collection of facts, dates and notable inventions. Rather, the story of hypertext serves as one of the primary ways in which the medium is explained, legitimated or, alternatively, dismissed by its various adherents, critics and practitioners. In this respect it is useful to keep Hayden White's notion of conceptual history in mind, which he defines as "a methodology of historical studies that focuses on the invention and development of the fundamental concepts underlying and informing a distinctly historical manner of being in the world."[1] For our purposes, what is notable here is the "development of the fundamental concepts" that inform hypertext's historical "being in the world." In other words, how is the historical narrative of hypertext constructed and what are the effects of this narrative on how hypertext is both understood and applied? To ask such questions is to probe the discursive nature of hypertext and thus enter into territories that are as much ideological as they are technical. The telling of the hypertext story, then, informs us more about the values, beliefs and predispositions of the "tellers" than it does about the objective "facts" of its development through time.

A cue can be taken here from Alex Galloway's recent book *Protocol* in which the Internet is probed via two fundamental questions: How does it work? and Whom does it work for? This leads us, as Eugene Thacker states in *Protocol*'s introduction, to the matter of praxis—"a set of procedures, actions and practices that are designed in particular ways to achieve particular ends in particular contexts."[2] Hypertext is thus not innocent; nor is it value free. It does certain things for certain people. The heart of hypertext, in other words, lies within its technical specifications because it is these specifications that drive the manner in which it is used and understood. However, these technical specifications did not fall from the sky. They are the explicit consequences of particular decisions, values, ideas and circumstances that are historically situated and, furthermore, than can often be connected to specific individuals and the choices they made at a particular time and in a particular place.

With this in mind, we can turn our attention to the history of hypertext that is not as straightforward as one might initially suspect. Despite being a relatively recent arrival, hypertext is often inserted into historical accounts that span hundreds, if not thousands, of years. This is in itself rather telling in so much that it speaks of a particular bias on the part of the academic community to situate hypertext within a particular historical trajectory. Typical genealogies of hypertext's predecessors include Egyptian hieroglyphics, Plato's *Phaedrus*, Laurence Sterne's *The Life and Opinions of Tristram Shandy*, Gutenberg's printing press, James Joyce's *Ulysses*, Jean-Paul Sartre's *What is Literature*, Raymond Queneau's *Oulipo (A Thousand Billion Poems)*, Marc Saporta's *Composition Number One*, Julio Cortazar's *Hopscotch* and just about anything by Jorge Luis Borges. Although potentially bewildering at first, such a massive historical sweep makes perfect sense if one thinks of hypertext as a stage or component of the overall history of writing technology itself. Consequently, hypertext must be juxtaposed with notable developments that include both specific technological landmarks, such as the printing press, and groundbreaking literary or creative works, such as Joyce's *Ulysses*, that extend the boundaries of writings formal and expressive possibilities.

The key concept here is that writing is a technology, an idea that Jay David Bolter pursued rigorously, especially in his nearly canonical book *Writing Space: Computers, Hypertext, and the Late Age of Print* that has recently been revised and retitled to accommodate his reevaluation of hypertext. Central to his methodology is a broad understanding of technology that includes "skills as well as machines" citing the etymological roots of *techne*, the Greek word used to indicate "a set of rules, system or method of making or doing, whether in the useful arts, or of the fine arts."[3] Bolter continues

> All the ancient arts and crafts had this in common: that the craftsman must develop a skill, a technical state of mind in using tools and materials. Ancient and modern writing are technologies in the sense that they are methods for arranging verbal ideas in a visual space. The writer always needs a surface on which to make his or her marks and a tool with which to make them, and these materials become part of the contemporary definition of writing.

The understanding of writing as a technology has an important bearing on how the history of hypertext is told and positioned. Hypertext, like the quill pen, the papyrus scroll and the printing press, is a technological form that requires certain skills and makes certain forms or types of expression more or less possible and natural. As Bolter notes, "writing technologies are never external agents that invade and occupy the minds of their users. These technologies are natural or naturalized only in the sense that they are constituted by the interaction of physical materials and human practices." Consequently, the introduction and adoption of a new writing technology sends complex tremors throughout the entire cultural and historical matrix that necessitate a reassessment of both past and present assumptions and practices. Katherine Hayles makes a comparable point in her evocative book *Writing Machines*, which is part of MIT's innovative Media Work series. Central to her approach and overall concern is an advocation of a "material" approach to the study of writing and media, which is to say that one needs to pay attention to the media within or upon which a particular narrative or story is embedded or realized. This may seem like an obvious point, but one has to consider that within literary studies, there is virtually no attention given to how the actual medium of the book, for instance, informs, reflects, shapes or otherwise influences the content. As students of literature we are encouraged to pay attention to only the content:

> It is becoming overwhelmingly clear that we can no longer afford to ignore the material basis of literary production. Materiality of the artifact can no longer be positioned as a subspeciality within literary studies; it must be central, for without it we have little hope of forging a robust and nuanced account of how literature is changing under the impact of information technologies.[4]

With all this said, where does the "straight history" of hypertext actually begin? If we take for granted the concept of writing as a technology and the need to focus on its material conditions, then a logical starting point would be with the actual invention of writing itself. However, to do so also requires a point of comparison; in other words, a historical stage where writing was not yet on the scene. Thus, we go back even further to the age of orality, as Walter Ong has termed it—an age where the primary mode of communication among human beings was via the spoken voice.[5] It is here that another curiosity arises. The features or characteristics of oral cultures are often favorably compared with the fundamental nature of hypertext. Consider, for example, the manner in which the ancient Greek poet Homer, a familiar paragon of the oral tradition, is associated with hypertext in this quote by Bolter:

> Homer's repetitive formulaic poetry is a forerunner of topographic writing in the electronic writing space. The Homeric poet wrote by putting together formulaic blocks, and the audience "read" his performance in terms of those blocks. The electronic writer and reader, programmer and user, do the same today. Like oral poetry and storytelling, electronic writing is a highly associative writing, in which the pattern of associations among verbal elements is as much as part of the text as the elements themselves.[6]

The term "associative" is key here, for it is via hypertext's apparent ability to tap into the human brain's preference for associative thinking that renders it a close cousin to the oral tradition, which is also understood as a culture that comprehended the world via the nonhierarchical mind-set of association. Such a historical return again implies as much about hypertext as it does about contemporary interpretations and assessments of ancient oral cultures. Many accounts of such cultures depict its citizens as living much closer to the natural rhythm of our planet and thus distanced from the usual trappings of the modern condition. As Harold Innis famously noted, oral cultures are "time bound," meaning that they are situated very much in the present rather than in the future, as is the case with contemporary societies.[7] Time-bound oral societies are often confined geographically, with an emphasis on collectivity and the common good. In marked contrast to space-bound cultures, which is the term Innis uses to describe our present age, time-bound cultures de-emphasize individualization and give preference to consensus, tradition and continuity. Space-bound cultures, on the other hand are driven by the relentless rationalism of literacy, individualization and the need for control and are thus prone to the evils of meaningless consumerism, impersonal social exchange and cultural hegemony. It is not difficult to see how such concepts could easily lend themselves to a kind of romantic idealism in which the "good old days" are frequently referred to as a means to lament about our present age. Against such a backdrop, hypertext emerges as a type of cultural hero in terms of its apparent ability to return something that has long been lost and, moreover, to usher in a set of paradigms with which to better comprehend our complex world.

More than the Book

The emergence of writing, and eventually the printed book, occupies a central position in the hypertext story by way of providing a concrete counterexample to the essence of hypertext. The book, in short, is almost everything that hypertext is not—permanent, inflexible, physical, unchangeable, linear and noninteractive. Pronouncements regarding the "end of the book" are thus relatively frequent, especially in articles written about hypertext for the popular press. Among the best known is Robert Coover's article "The End of Books" published in the *New York Times Book Review* in 1992.[8] Coover's article and his subsequent review of various hypertext novels, also for the *New York Times*, introduced the medium to a wider public and arguably served as a spur for various negative reactions to the book's apparent demise. Among these is Sven Birkerts's book, *The Gutenberg Elegies: The Fate of Reading in an Electronic Age*, which laments the demise of conventional literacy and our culture's ever-increasing fascination with mass media and entertainment.

It is with this concept of the book's limits that the historical narrative of hypertext often turns to efforts by writers to challenge the conventions imposed by the printed page. Modernist art and literature provide the most common touchstone in this regard, especially those works that tend to present radical departures from normative approaches to narrative structure, realism and layout. What is again implicated here is the concept of hypertext as being a continuation of an identifiable historical trajectory. In other words, hypertext is a logical extension of the print culture by virtue of providing tangible solutions to the limits of linear narrative and the printed page. Bolter's designation of the "late age of print" captures this idea nicely and serves as a clear example of how hypertext is often constructed around a type of evolutionary narrative. Hypertext is where the future of narrative and knowledge lies. Now, it must be acknowledged that more recent writings on hypertext, such as Bolter's revised edition of *Writing Space* and J. Yellowlees Douglas's *The End of Books or Books Without End*, offer a reassessment of hypertext as a sign of things to come. Bolter in particular is much more hesitant of making predictions about the future, noting the need to eliminate "many prophetic claims that either did not come true or were simply made irrelevant by the development of hypertext in directions that I had not foreseen."[9] Douglas acerbically notes that much of the "hand-waving and hand-wringing about interactive narratives" is based on often idealized or imaginary encounters with works of hypertext as opposed to close and careful readings. "More bizarrely, pieces in recent scholarly journals have attempted to survey the strengths and weaknesses of the field with nary a mention of a specific writer, text, or concrete example."[10] Although such a lack of academic rigor could simply be seen as a sign of laziness and a desire to keep at least an ill-formed finger on the pulse of contemporary trends, the tendency for critics to engage in uninformed evaluations of hypertext is also indicative of the allure of the aforementioned techno-evolutionism. Hypertext (and technology in general) seem to invite prophesy, prediction and ruminations of the future on the part of those encountering the medium, even if only in passing. The historical narrative of hypertext is thus one that celebrates rupture, transition and revolution in an attempt to validate the claim that it is the next evolutionary stage in the overall history of human communication.

Founding Figures: Bush, Nelson and Engelbart

The history of hypertext is, of course, not limited to the grand narratives that sweep over millennia with apparent ease and lack of detail. Hypertext is also the product of identifiable technological developments and thus is attributable to specific innovators and historical developments.[11] The most common starting point for the technological emergence of hypertext is Vannevar Bush's oft-quoted article "As We May Think" published by the *Atlantic Monthly* in 1945. In this article Bush engaged in a type of thought experiment through which he proposed the development of a personalized database that he called the "memex":

> Consider a future device for individual use, which is a sort of mechanised private file and library. It needs a name, and to coin one at random, "memex" will do. A memex is a device in which an individual stores all his books, records and communications, and which is mechanised so that it may be consulted with exceeding speed and flexibility. It is an enlarged intimate supplement to his memory.[12]

Technically, the memex was envisioned as a combination of mechanical devices, microfilm photography and photocells and thus very much in the domain of analog information technology. On the surface it has the appearance of a large desk and is, in fact, conceived of by Bush as being "primarily a piece of furniture."[13] Thus it resonates with familiarity and also follows the early practice of designing technological devices for the home as furniture pieces. The complexity and radicalism of its machinations were to be properly contained behind comforting shells of polished wood and decorative embellishments.

The significance and continued relevance of the memex, however, is not limited to its technical details, despite its still admirable ingenuity. What is important about the memex is largely a conceptual matter. "It [memex] affords an immediate step, however, to associative indexing, the basic idea of which is a provision whereby any item may be caused at will to select immediately and automatically another. This is the essential feature of the memex. The process of tying two items together."[14] This process of "tying two items together" would allow a memex user to create an associative trail of multiple documents or screens that could be produced through the entire body of the information contained within the memex. This trail would be unique to the individual who had constructed them and would, moreover, parallel in some fashion the individual's patterns of thought, memory and sense of narrative. In this fashion, the memex becomes more than just a mechanical aid but rather an "enlarged intimate supplement to memory."

Such a symbiosis between the mind and the machine is a familiar motif within the hypertext story, and indeed Bush's article has done its part in creating the historical precedent for such a conviction. In his more speculative moments, Bush in fact envisions the memex as enacting a form of intellectual immortality that would allow one to access the minds of past generations:

> The race progresses as the experience and reasoning of one generation is handed on to the next. Can a son inherit the memex of his father, or the disciple that of his master, refined and polished over the years, and go on from there? In this way can we avoid some of the loss which comes when oxygen is no longer furnished to the brain of the great thinker, when all the pattern of neurons so painstakingly refined becomes merely a mass of protein and nucleic acid? Can the race thus develop leaders, of such power of intellect, and such

> forces of conviction, that the world can be saved from its follies? Can science and technology, as they support and extend man's power of thought, bring us nearer to social wisdom, rather than merely to extend the control over the forces of nature for good or ill? This is an objective, of far greater importance than the conquest of disease, even than the conquest of mental aberrations.[15]

Bush's call to employ technology to "extend man's power of thought" is one heeded by Theodor Nelson and Douglas Engelbart who are both pioneers in terms of bringing hypertext into the real world of development and application. Both men cite Bush's memex as an important inspiration for their particular approaches to technology. In the case of Theodor Nelson who, in fact, coined the term hypertext, the computer was a veritable "freedom machine" that, if used correctly, is nothing short of the great emancipator of humanity capable of advancing not only knowledge, understanding and liberty but also the levels and possibilities of human artistry and skill.[16] Moreover, Nelson believed that hypertext held the additional potential to save the world from the tyranny of the book (and the stale world of academia that stands behind it)—a prospect that Nelson expounds with considerable frequency:

> The world of ideas is carved into territories, and assigned as fiefdoms to individuals who represented these territories (called Subjects); these lords and ladies in turn impose their own style and personality on them. The pupil must pay homage to the Duchess of History, the Count of Mathematics; and if you and these individuals do not like each other, you will almost surely dislike the subjects they control, which take on their stamp and personality. Each feudal lord has absolute power to bore, offend, and sever access.[17]

Nelson is not someone who thinks small. For him, hypertext promises revolution on a grand scale and indeed much of his life has been driven by his concentrated desire to bring "true hypertext" to the world. Much of Nelson's energies were and still are devoted to his project entitled, Xanadu, which is a culmination of many years of thinking and writing about using the computer as a new means to organize thought and engender alternative forms of expression and creativity. Born in 1937, Theodor Holms Nelson's vision of hypertext took root during his years as a Masters student at Harvard during the early 1960s. His embryonic ideas regarding the computer's revolutionary potential were first inscribed in his first book "Truth, Man and Choice," which he was unable to publish. Nelson attributed his failure to gain an audience for his ideas to his inability to properly organize his myriad of ideas via the artificial conventions of linear textuality. "You take a structured complex of thought (I like to call it a structangle) that you are trying to communicate, and you break it into individual sequential parts that can be put end to end, and this is a wholly artificial process, a breakdown not intrinsic to the structure of thought you are trying to convey, but based upon the fact that it has to be published eventually in a sequence."[18] This difficulty with the "preposterous extrinsic activity of taking the structure of thought and breaking it into pieces" that characterizes linear writing prompted Nelson to pursue other alternatives. This led to his first computer project, "The Thousand Theories Program," that modestly proposed to present a thousand different viewpoints about the whole of human knowledge. This project was essentially the precursor to Nelson's conception of hypertext—a term he coined after he "realized the historical importance of choosing the right word for this new kind of text that would reshape the world."

The essential definition was unusually brief—"by hypertext I mean nonsequential writing."[19] The major characteristics at this point included the idea of branching texts, the ability to present "deep alternatives in the organization of the same material" and the necessary constructs or structures for the organization of the hypertext system. Nelson also identifies six types of hypertexts. The first is "basic or chunk style hypertext" that follows the "footnote" model of branching off from the main text. Second, the typology of "collateral hypertext" is similar but more extensive in that it allows for "compound annotations or parallel texts." The third category "stretchtext" is one of continuous change—a change that is controlled by the reader by way of "throttles" that not only move the text around the screen but also control its "growth":

> There are a screen and two throttles. The first throttle moves the text forward and backward, up and down on the screen. The second throttle causes changes in the writing itself: throttling toward you causes the text to become longer by minute degrees. Gaps appear between phrases; new words and phrases pop into the gaps, an item at a time. Push back on the throttle and the writing becomes shorter and less detailed.[20]

From this point, things begin to expand. An "anthological hypertext" consists of materials from a wide range of sources in a manner similar to that of a conventional anthology. The "grand hypertext" follows closely behind but, given the name, is far more extensive. Typically, it is to include "everything written about a subject or vaguely relevant about it, tied together by editors ... in which you may read in all the directions you wish to pursue."[21] At the very top of Nelson's list is "the real dream" that is nothing sort of *everything* being included in one sweeping hypertext. Nelson predicted, with his customary self-assurance, that hypertext was soon destined to replace the printed word.

Nelson's newly christened term made its public debut in Cleveland in a conference paper presented to the Association for Computing Machinery. Its reception, according to Nelson, was enthusiastic but short lived. "From there it was downhill, downhill for years, and then decades." It seemed that no one understood the far-reaching essence of his idea—a problem that he attributed to a clash of paradigms. Borrowing from Thomas Kuhn, Nelson saw paradigms as ideas "too big to get through the door," ideas that were more than ideas but rather essential aspects of an entire world of perception, opinion and ideas. People are contained within paradigms and thus act and believe in accordance with the view afforded by the vantage point of such an enclosure. Nelson, thus, found himself standing at the door with his paradigm for a new literature unable to go beyond the threshold. He had little choice but to stand there, waving his arms and ideas about in mid-air.

It was not until the late 1970s, some time after his publication of *Computer Lib/Dream Machines*, that Nelson began to assemble in earnest a working organization dedicated to bringing Xanadu, the ultimate hypertext, into the world.[22] Before that time, project Xanadu had more or less been a solitary effort, realized primarily in written articles and books rather than in actual computer environments.

The goals of Douglas Engelbart are no less modest than those of Nelson. He too wished to harness the power of the computer to raise humanity to a new level of existence, or in his words to "invest the rest of my heretofore aimless career toward making the most difference in improving the lot of the human race."[23] His desire to make a difference was eventually formalized in both conceptual and practical projects aimed at "augmenting human intellect." A number of these projects and visions are directly related to many of the information tools we use today, notably the computer mouse, graphical interfaces (such as Windows), videoconferencing, the Internet and word processing, to name just a few of the more common applications. Indeed, Engelbart has been hailed as one of the great inventors of the twentieth century whose concepts and inventions, whether realized or not, continue to have a profound impact on contemporary society and culture. His specific contribution to hypertext is most readily associated with his development of mixed text/graphic displays, the mouse and the hyperlink. Many of these developments are outlined in his now canonical report "Augmenting Human Intellect: A Conceptual Framework" and the film documentation of a demonstration at Stanford University in 1968, sometimes referred to as the "mother of all demos."[24] Engelbart, in short, was responsible for inventing many of the actual tools and programming concepts that are integral to today's hypertext systems. Like Bush and Nelson, Engelbart also helped to solidify the conceptual paradigms and assumptions regarding the values and potentials of human–computer interaction.

Pioneers and Programs: Intermedia, HyperCard, Storyspace and Voyager

The history of hypertext could not be complete without acknowledging the tremendous amount of work done at Brown University, starting around 1961 and continuing at a somewhat reduced pace until today. Among the principal figures is Andries van Dam who joined the faculty at Brown in 1965, and who led many of the initiatives in the development of sophisticated hypermedia applications, notably the Hypertext Editing Systems (HES) and the File Retrieval Editing System (FRESS), the latter of which had a relatively long history of use. In 1985, Norman Meyrowitz founded the Brown's Institute for Research in Information and Scholarship (IRIS), which developed a software platform known as Intermedia. Briefly, the Intermedia is a hypermedia system intended for use within university research and teaching and is described as providing "a framework for object-oriented, direct manipulation editors and applications, and the capability to link together materials created with those applications."[25] Among the applications embedded within the Intermedia system were a text editor, a graphics editor, a scanned image viewer, a three-dimensional object viewer and a timeline editor. Whereas such interrelated software environments are increasingly common today, what was significant about Intermedia at the time was that any number of these applications could be opened on the desktop at a time and users were able to work easily within a truly integrated multimedia environment where documents created in one application could be linked to those created in another. Another notable feature of Intermedia was the ability to link between specific points or locations within a given document rather than just linking to documents in their entirety, which was common practice among other early hypermedia systems.

The proof of the Intermedia pudding, so to speak, lies of course in its actual application and use. As part of Brown's research in hypertext, Intermedia was used in a number of undergraduate courses, with one of the notable (and actually still surviving) examples being the "Victorian Web," a resource hypertext created for an undergraduate English Literature course by George Landow. With the demise of Intermedia, the Victorian Web was transferred to Storyspace in 1992 and then to the Web in 1994.[26] True to the hypertext ideal of collaboration, the Victorian Web invites and includes contributions from the public although any submission is subject to scrutiny by Landow, who continues to be involved in the project. To this day, Landow's Victorian Web still serves as a valuable benchmark for appreciating and understanding the significance of hypertext with respect to matters of education and reading/writing in general.[27]

Apple Computer occupies a special place within the history of hypertext with the release of the program HyperCard in 1986, which was one of the first hypertext editing systems available to the general public. Included with the purchase of every Macintosh, HyperCard was based on the metaphor of a stack of virtual index cards. Each card was made up of two basic components: fields that could store data and background that determined the pattern and layout for each card. These backgrounds were extremely versatile for the time and could include anything from text, images, text and picture editors and sound. HyperCard allowed its users to create interactive databases via an easy-to-use computer language called HyperTalk that was closely patterned after the English language.

User interaction is achieved by clicking on the various "buttons" within a particular card. The buttons can be programmed to perform a variety of actions such as the playing of sounds, opening new stacks or taking the user to different places within a particular stack. The ease and relative sophistication of HyperCard quickly created a large and surprisingly loyal group of enthusiasts who quickly learned how to use HyperTalk to create a variety of applications that ranged from the practical to the bizarre. What was particularly empowering about the program was the fact that it introduced programming to a wider public, meaning that users with relatively little computer experience could actively design their own interactive environments. HyperCard is also recognized as introducing the concept of multimedia to the general public and indeed served as the platform from which Apple developed its own directions in multimedia software and development. However, as is often typical within the computer industry, Apple did not quite understand or appreciate the significance of HyperCard and thus never fully took advantage of its potential. The program languished on the back burner for several years, primarily because of its creator Bill Atkinson's insistence that the program remain free of charge. The notion of free software did not sit well with a company dedicated to the profit model. HyperCard did eventually make it to a 3.0 version, but only in beta form and was thus never released to the wider public. That said, HyperCard still commands loyalty from a modest group of enthusiasts around the world, many of whom are associated with the International HyperCard User Group (IHUG) whose Web site consistently praises the merits of HyperCard as well as serves as a vehicle to convince Apple to reactivate development of the program.[28]

The various incarnations of hypertext—whether imaginary as in the case of the memex or applied as with HyperCard or Intermedia—all speak to one of the central mantras of the hypertext "doctrine," namely the blurring together of the conventional roles of the author and the reader. "Intermedia is both an author's tool and a reader's tool. The system, in fact, makes no distinction between types of users. ... Creating new materials and making and following links are all integrated into a single seamless, multiuser environment."[29] Such an amalgamation of the reader/writer also ties into the notion of hypertext as being paradigmatic in nature. In other words, hypertext in addition to providing a practical tool also provides a fundamental theoretical model with which to reassess and perhaps even overturn prior models of or approaches to the organization of information, human-computer interaction and the very nature of self-expression itself. As part of the Hypertext 96 conference proceedings, for instance, researchers Nürnberg, Leggett, Schneider and Schanse not only confirmed hypertext's role "as either a paradigm for human-computer interaction or information organization," but also argued that hypermedia provides a new paradigm for computing itself—"one in which human-computer interaction, information storage and retrieval, programming, and control are integrated in a common conceptual framework."[30] For our purposes, it is the reference to the "common conceptual framework" that is of interest here. Once again, hypertext is more than just a new tool. It is rather a finite and identifiable body of principles, visions, systems and beliefs that offer a viable and concrete alternative to previous modes of organization, writing, reading and thinking.

In addition to the development of applications, the history of hypertext was also driven by efforts to create hypermedia content for the wider public. Two companies stand out here, the first being the long-standing Eastgate Systems and the other the somewhat legendary Voyager Company that, sadly, no longer exists. Eastgate Systems describes itself as a company dedicated to "serious hypertext," and despite never having reached any substantial commercial success is widely recognized as one of the main bastions for the creative uses of hypertext media. Central to Eastgate Systems' success and longevity is its hypertext authoring program Storyspace that was premiered at the first ACM hypertext workshop in November 1987 by Michael Joyce, David Bolter and John B. Smith using Joyce's canonical hyperfiction *Afternoon* as the vehicle to demonstrate Storyspace's potential.[31] As indicated by its name, Storyspace employs spatial metaphors to organize and present its content. Basically, a Storyspace hypertext "consists of nodes, or writing spaces, that are connected by directed links" employing the term "writing space" to represent "chunks of writings: facts, ideas, references, or entire passages" that are to be conceived as "tangible objects—things you pick up, arrange, and rearrange as your ideas change or as you discover new information."[32] Of course "writing" is not limited to only textual information as Storyspace, like many applications today, can easily accommodate visuals, animations and sound. To create links between any elements, a user has simply to draw a line between one object and another, which again grounds the Storyspace experience via spatial paradigms. Among its distinctive features is the Storyspace map, which is a mechanism that allows users to view and control the overall organization of a particular hypertext (Figure 1).

These maps may or may not be visible to readers, depending on the author's wishes. Indeed, another of Storyspace's distinctive features is the ability for writers to control how readers access a given hypertext via several reading templates, as is shown in Figure 2.

In addition to creating and distributing Storyspace, Eastgate Systems is the only major publisher of literary hyperfiction; indeed, the bulk of what is considered "serious" or worthy of any critical attention has been published by Eastgate. Some of the more widely known titles include Michael Joyce's *Afternoon*, Stuart

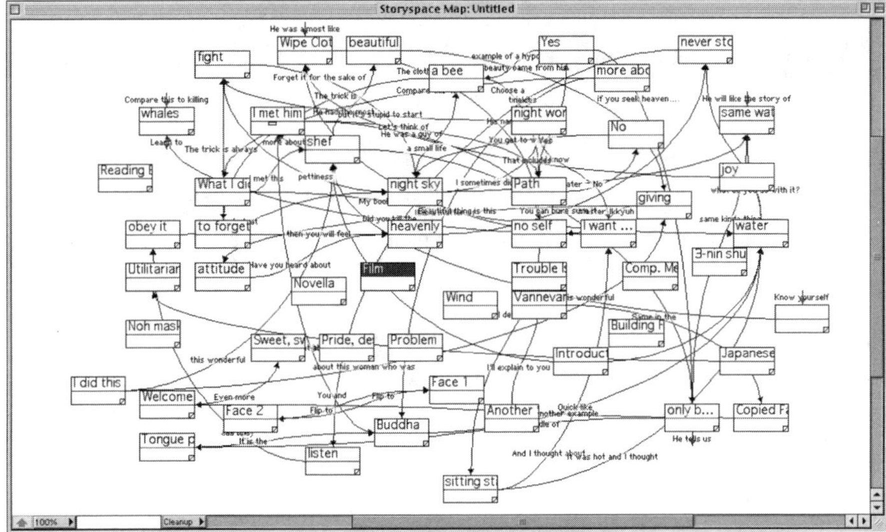

Figure 1. Storyspace map view.

Moulthrop's *Victory Garden*, Shelley Jackson's *Patchwork Girl*, John McDaid's *Uncle Buddy's Phantom Funhouse* and Judy Malloy's *Its Name Was Penelope*.[33] Many of these works are highly experimental in nature and, to varying degrees, could be said to follow or build upon the conventions and traditions of modern and postmodern literature, a topic that will be pursued in more depth in Chapter 2. For the moment, however, what can be said about Storyspace with respect to such experiments is the manner in which the software is considered as offering a viable and powerful alternative to other writing conventions and practices, notably print. Hypertext author Michael Joyce notes that "the medium of print expects writing to be hierarchical in structure and (with some important exceptions) linear in presentation. Yet text generation and invention is characterized by a multiplicity of relationships among ideas. When we move toward formal organization, we are closing off options for ourselves as writers and for our readers."[34] The strength of Storyspace is said to lie in its ability to assist writers in constructively working with multiplicity, offering in a sense a writing space that allows one to take advantage of the tangential nature of human thought and the creative process in general. Accordingly, Storyspace is seen as a more fluid and dynamic environment that does not restrict cognitive processes as severely as the conventions of linear print. As part of Eastgate's testimonial page, writer Kim Arnold praises Storyspace as being "the most fertile, flexible, giving, nurturing place I have ever found to write in. I love this space!" Equally enthusiastic is George Landow who describes the software as "the finest hypertext system in

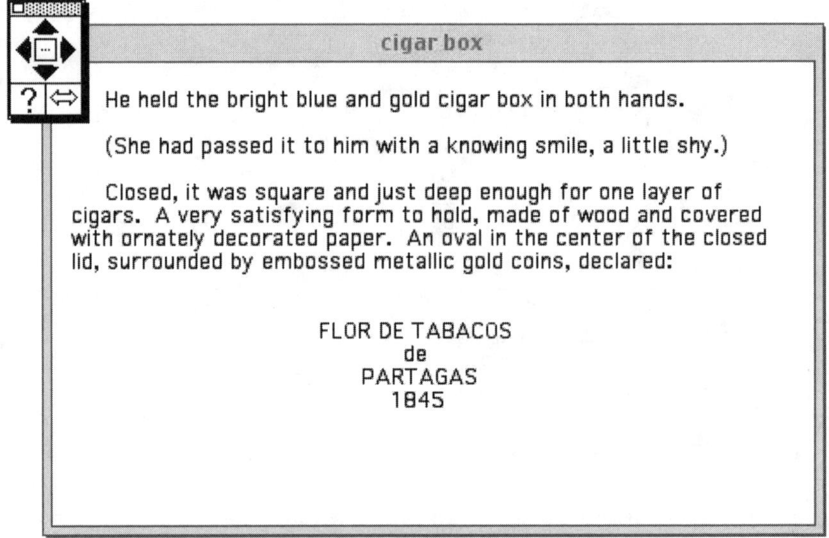

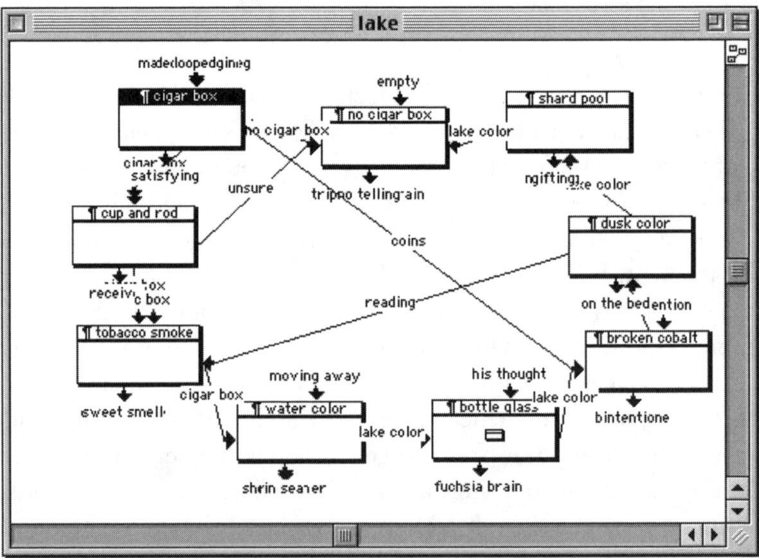

Figure 2. Screenshots of Carolyn Guyer's *Quibbling*. The first displays the lexia "cigar box," and the second the overall "map view" of the "lake" section. Authors have the choice of whether or not to allow readers to access the map view.

existence ... [the system] that most fulfills the dreams of hypertext visionaries."[35] Such claims essentially position Storyspace as a valuable friend to the writer or creative individual in so much that it becomes a collaborative agent in the creative process. In this way, Storyspace echoes Bush's vision in terms of the program becoming "intimate" with the user, so to speak. Such a melding of mind and machine speaks to the aspects of cyborg theory that probes the manner in which the merger of humans and technology potentially open up new possibilities that lie outside of the terrains of either the purely human or the purely technological.

The Voyager Corporation, founded by visionary Bob Stein in 1984, is generally acknowledged as a milestone in multimedia publishing and, moreover, as a company that was well ahead of its time. Originally created to release classic movies on laser disks, Voyager soon devoted itself to the creation of multimedia CD-ROMs and later Expanded Books—the term used to describe its electronic versions of existing books.[36] The first of the CD-ROM projects was "Beethoven: Symphony No. 9," which is generally acknowledged as the first multimedia CD-ROM of any real significance, both technically and in terms of popularity.[37] With the relative success of this release, Voyager gradually added to its catalog of eclectic and innovative titles that ranged from multimedia versions of *Macbeth* to the Beatles. What distinguished Voyager almost right from the beginning was its willingness to take on projects that were not solely geared to the bottom line and the mass market. "While much of the CD-ROM content business concentrates on generating hit entertainment titles, Voyager's sensibilities are closer to that of the print publisher. ... Stein's creative stable includes performance artist Laurie Anderson, scientists Stephen Jay Gould, AI guru Marvin Minsky, musical innovators The Residents, and Pedro Meyer, one of Latin American's most recognized photographers."[38]

Like other pioneers, Stein's vision of Voyager's purpose and ultimate mission is anything but small. "The subtext of what's happening is that we are changing the way that humans communicate with each other. ... This profound shift is more significant than the invention of the printing press, and the deep implications of it won't be known for some time. A thousand years from now, humanity will look back at the late part of the twentieth century as the time when something big started."[39] While one may smirk at the somewhat grandiose nature of Stein's claims, there is no denying that the emergence of digital publishing, whether text, music or video, has indeed changed the industry as a whole and, perhaps more importantly, the habits and expectations of consumers. At the heart of his vision are the particulars of the expanded book concept that was later developed into something called "the expanded book toolkit" that was a product aimed primarily at publishers interested in releasing titles in new media.[40] The first three Expanded Books, which sold at a modest price of $19.95 each, were *Alice in Wonderland*, Douglas Adam's *Hitchhiker's Guide to the Galaxy* and Michael Crichton's *Jurassic Park*. Modeled after the format and aesthetics of actual print books, Expanded Books are HyperCard stacks that capitalize on the computer's ability to index and search information as well as its ability to incorporate a variety of media formats, notably sound and moving images. The interface allows users to see how far they have progressed in a book via a "progress gauge," the ability to annotate a text via a notes function and to highlight sections of text. The program also allows users to search a given text, build and save their own indexes and to retrace their steps through a particular Expanded Book. Although such features are not exactly revolutionary, especially when juxtaposed against the more elaborate paradigms of Eastgate Systems or even the visions of Ted Nelson, Voyager's Expanded Books are still recognized as a crucial attempt in bringing multimedia publishing to the general public. In his review of the software, Jim Ottaviani favorably compares Eastgate's approach to the "Gutenberg Principle," which "advocates making the smallest incremental changes possible when introducing a new technology":

> Gutenburg did this by printing only in a Gothic font matched as closely as he could to what monks used. (He needed 300 different characters to do this.) Only later did he use other typefaces. By explicitly adopting the print book as their metaphor, Voyager has made the smallest possible incremental change.[41]

What Ottaviani is suggesting here is that Voyager's strength lies precisely in its ability to build and modestly depart from the conventional paradigms of print technology, which is in marked contrast to the strategy employed by Eastgate Systems and the many authors making use of Storyspace as a means to write creative fiction. Ironically, Voyager was unable to sustain itself economically and ceased to be a viable company in 1995 whereas Eastgate Systems, though small, continues to thrive.[42]

The success and longevity of hypertext is to a large degree dependent upon its contextualization within a particular community of experts, developers and enthusiasts. As such, another important milestone in the history of hypertext is the first official Hypertext Conference (known as Hypertext 87), which was held at Chapel Hill University in Illinois from November 13 to 15, 1987. The list of presenters at this inaugural conference reads like a who's who list in the hypertext universe: Ted Nelson, Jay Bolter, George Landow, Michael Joyce, Andries van Dam, Douglas Engelbart to name only a few. In addition to pioneering luminaries, the conference also featured influential technological systems, including Apple's HyperCard, Intermedia, Guide and Storyspace. Although not the only conference or society concerned with hypertext, the annual "Conference on Hypertext and Hypermedia" (HT) is definitely the most long standing and high profile of academic societies and, as such, presents a major portal for the continuing development of hypertext as a technical and social phenomenon. Not surprisingly, given the nature of hypertext, HT is relatively interdisciplinary in nature, with one of the primary aims being to bring "together scholars, researchers, and practitioners from diverse disciplines to consider the form, role and impact of hypertext and hypermedia."[43] Equally familiar is the emphasis on investigating "the transformative power of hypermedia and its ability to alter the way we read, write, argue, work, exchange information and entertain ourselves." The emphasis on hypertext's "transformative power" is notable in that it resonates with many of the already mentioned claims regarding its ability to enact fundamental change, more so when compared with other technorevolutionary forces, such as the invention of writing or the printing press. That said, the numerous papers, presentation and demonstrations that have been delivered since HT 1987 hardly represent a unified voice. As in any healthy academic society, debates and disagreements are the norm and HT remains a vital context within which to measure the pulse of contemporary developments and trends in hypermedia.

Everyday Hypertext: The World Wide Web

For most people, the term and the concept of hypertext are synonymous with the World Wide Web (WWW) and, indeed, if one were to measure the success of hypertext, then the millions who make use of the Web on a daily basis would testify to its social, economic and political import. Hypertext, at least when considered as the means with which the Internet is conventionally accessed, has become a part of the mainstream, for better or worse.

The history of the World Wide Web and the Internet is a tale well and often told in publications concerned with digital media and the social impact of computing technology and, as such, it is not necessary to reproduce the full account here. Nevertheless, a few salient characteristics, concepts, contexts and phenomena are worth mentioning again within the context of this chapter. To begin with, there is the matter of the Internet's military roots to contend with. Much has been made about the fact that today's Internet is the child of the cold war and was designed to withstand the destructive force of nuclear war. The key design elements were decentralization and redundancy, which as Alex Galloway notes function as polar opposites to the essence of nuclear war:

> If one can consider nuclear attack as the most highly energetic, dominating, and centralized force that one knows—an archetype of the modern era—then the Net is at once the solution to and inversion of this massive material threat, for it is precisely noncentralized, nondominating, and nonhostile. ... In fact, the reason why the Internet would withstand nuclear attack is precisely because its internal protocols are the enemy of bureaucracy, of rigid hierarchy, and of centralization.[44]

The idea of the Internet as being such a polar opposite to all that is centralized, linear and hierarchical resonates well with the overall concept of hypertext insomuch that in both cases the material structure, so to speak, is key to the overall function and effect. Of particular import is the notion that decentralization is presented and structured as a form of empowerment insomuch that it literally resists and combats the forces of centralization. For military strategists, of course, this was hardly seen as a means to challenge the status quo and promote a culture of free, unregulated expression. Yet for those of a more revolutionary mind-set, the Internet (and the Web) is presented as a potential tool with which to dismantle rigid social structures and replace them with a society of open and free exchange.[45] Herein lies the great paradox of the Internet and to some extent digital media in general. On the one hand there is a structural basis for decentralized, nonlinear and uncontrollable information flow and social organization. Yet, on the other hand, never before in the history of humanity has there existed a technological infrastructure that is as capable of tracking, regulating, processing and controlling the way in which we exchange capital and ideas.

Technically speaking, hypertext is more closely associated with the World Wide Web given the fact that it is built upon the protocols of Hypertext Transfer Protocol (HTTP) and Hypertext Markup Language (HTML). The driving force behind the origins of the WWW is Tim Berners-Lee who, during his time at CERN (the European Organization for Nuclear Research), developed the system as a means to help members of the physics community share information with one another. The year 1989 can be considered as the birth of the WWW, for it was then that Berners-Lee "proposed that a global hypertext space be created in which any network-accessible information could be referred to by a single Universal Document Identifier."[46] The first actual Web server, which ran on the NeXT computer created by Apple pioneer Steven Jobs, was made available to the High Energy Physics community in the summer of 1991. This original server (whose address was info.cern.ch) soon began to strain under the pressure of an increasing number of visitors. In response, Berners-Lee created the World Wide Web Consortium in September 1994 that he describes as "a neutral open forum where companies and organizations to whom the future of the Web is important come to discuss and to agree on new common computer protocols. It has been a center for issue raising, design, and decision by consensus and also a fascinating vantage point from which to view that evolution." The World Wide Web, however, was not merely the result of Berners-Lee's desire to create a more efficient means to disseminate information. He too was driven by a vision:

> The dream behind the Web is of a common information space in which we communicate by sharing information. Its universality is essential: the fact that a hypertext link can point to anything, be it personal, local or global, be it draft or highly polished. There was

> a second part of the dream, too, dependent on the Web being so generally used that it became a realistic mirror (or in fact the primary embodiment) of the ways in which we work and play and socialize. That was that once the state of our interactions was on line, we could then use computers to help us analyze it, make sense of what we are doing, where we individually fit in, and how we can better work together.

Berners-Lee's comments are telling for a number of reasons. First is the aspiration to create a universal system that can literally be accessed from anywhere and, moreover, can ultimately contain all forms of knowledge in whatever form. Second is the desire for the Web to become a "realistic mirror" of human interaction and communication itself—a desire that points to the relatively long-standing emphasis on the computer as being more than just a tool but rather an integral part of our very social (and perhaps even physical) makeup.

However, it was not until Marc Andreessen and Eric Bina created the browser "Mosaic" in 1992, which unlike other browsers at the time allowed images and text to appear on the same page. Equally innovative was the ability to embed hyperlinks within a document, meaning that users had simply to click on a link to access a new document. This was in marked contrast to earlier systems that employed reference numbers that users had to type in manually. Mosaic was almost an instant success and due to its rising popularity Andreessen and Bina quickly created versions that could run on Windows and Macintosh platforms. By 1993, Mosaic had reached a level of significance that it warranted coverage in the business sections for both the *New York Times* and the *Guardian*. His studies complete, Andreessen moved from Illinois to Palo Alto, California, where with the help of Silicon Graphics founder Jim Clark set up the Mosaic Communications Corporation. The primary mission of the company was to build on the success of Mosaic and to create a new product that would be vastly superior. A new name was created—Netscape—that upon its first release on October 13, 1994, took the world of the Web by storm. It became the browser of choice and soon gained an unprecedented level of ubiquity. However, Netscape was unable to retain its dominance and was soon replaced by Microsoft's Explorer as the world's most popular browser. Netscape was eventually bought out by America Online in 1999, which seemed to have little interest in the browser in terms of product development until relatively recently.

The Bias of Hypertext

Browser wars aside, what is significant about the World Wide Web in terms of the concerns of this book is that it represents how most of us experience hypertext on a day-to-day basis. Given this fact, a number of important issues are raised that in effect bring us back to the various questions posed at the beginning of this chapter. To rephrase, what does the WWW, as a manifestation of hypertext, reveal in terms of its social, political and cultural bias? What and who are favored by the Web? To what extent does the Web compromise or extend the more visionary or radical concepts of hypertext?

One manner with which to approach such questions is through Andrew Feenberg's concept of "technical code" that he describes as the "background of unexamined cultural assumptions literally designed into the technology itself."[47] This background of assumptions is a crucial mix of values, ideas, concepts and cultural norms that are essentially part of the technology itself both in terms of material form and application. A given piece of technology, such as a Palm Pilot, for instance, is thus more than a handy new tool but rather a discursive and ideological object that speaks to the cultural, economic and political voices that went into its creation. What does the Palm Pilot "say"? For one it is a testimony to the changing nature and experience of space and time in the twenty-first century where the boundaries between work and leisure time have blurred into one constantly connected present. Second, it speaks also of the dominant values of our postmodern, post-industrial information society where mobility, access, media convergence, information and time management are paramount for a socially and economically successful life. Accordingly, the Palm Pilot and a host of other technologies effectively confirm the values and mind-sets of the dominant social order, which in the case of most Western societies can be represented by global capitalism. For Feenberg, this means that the technical code can be linked to what is known as the hegemonic forces within a society, which is another way of describing these dominant values that determine, often "invisibly," how we live out our day-to-day lives.

> Capitalist social and technical requirements are thus condensed in a "technological rationality" or a "regime of truth" which brings the construction and interpretation of technical systems into conformity with the requirements of a system of domination. I will call this phenomenon the social code of technology or, more briefly, the technical code of capitalism. Capitalist hegemony, on this account, is an effect of its code.[48]

To some, Feenberg may seem to be overstating his case, especially through the use of such loaded terms as "conformity" and "domination." Most of us, I think, would balk at the notion that we are controlled by our technologies or that we are all just pawns in a world ruled by evil capitalists. However, it is important to consider how Feenberg is using such terms and also how concepts such as "power" and "capitalism" are being framed within his argument. Similar to another philosopher,

Michael Foucault, concepts such as power, capitalism, conformity and domination are not necessarily being employed as negative terms but rather as descriptive indicators of how the world works. Consider, for example, the concept of "power" as used to describe human relationships. To a large degree the manner in which we define and understand our relationships with one another is based on a balance of power: a mother has power over her child in a manner that she can control the child's circumstances in order to make sure that the child avoids injury, learns important skills and so forth. One could describe teacher-student or doctor-patient relationships on a similar basis. Even a simple friendship is structured by power relationships in which one friend may take on certain "roles" that grant him a measure of "authority" over activities and exchanges. In terms of technology, similar mechanisms are at work insomuch that "social purposes are 'embodied' in the technology" and are, thus, more than just the practical results of a neutral tool:

> The embodiment of specific purposes is achieved through the "fit" of the technology and its social environment. The technical ideas combined in the technology are neutral, but the study of any specific technology can trace in it the impress of a mesh of social determinations which preconstruct a whole domain of social activity aimed at definite social goals.[49]

What then are the technical codes of hypertext and more specifically what does the history of hypertext tell us about the meaning and potential direction of such codes? Think back to the topics covered in this chapter's brief historical overview:

1. The oral/literate distinction and the manner in which hypertext is often linked to certain characteristics of the oral tradition as well as compared to the revolutionary impact of the first printing press.
2. The tendency to situate the creative use of hypertext within the experimental traditions of modern and postmodern literature.
3. Vannevar Bush and the memex.
4. The visions of pioneers such as Ted Nelson, Douglas Engelbart and Andries van Dam.
5. Equally pioneering applications such as Intermedia, Storyspace, HyperCard and Mosaic.
6. The use of hypertext by publishers, educators and creative writers and how such individuals describe and characterize such use.

In the first case hypertext as a technology is often linked to a particular historical trajectory that for the most part is progressive in nature. In other words, hypertext represents an important evolutionary development that is not only more appropriate for current conditions but also represents a marked improvement over previous technologies and practices. Accordingly, like the transition from oral to written communication or the introduction of the printing press, hypertext is in many ways a radical break, the new medium on the block that will take those who employ it to new expressive heights. One part of hypertext's technical code is thus an ongoing sequence of evolutionary development that, as Jody Berland identifies, effectively characterizes technology as a self-evolving system that essentially has a life and mandate of its own:

> The conflation of human and technological evolution works not only to envision electrifying futures but also to displace alternate strategies for imagining our futures. Techno-evolutionism displaces alternate imaginings by posting the technological imperative as coming from outside ourselves, outside of human culture, through a self-generating evolutionary progression rather than from the culpable logics of our own social system.[50]

One of the more observable outcomes of "techno-evolutionism" is the palpable excitement and revolutionary zeal of many hypertext advocates who more often than not are more enthralled by hypertext's future potential than with what is actually possible within a given social and technological context. Equally pertinent, as Berland identifies, is the notion that hypertext is in part driven by forces that are "outside" of our explicit control or ability to fully appreciate and understand. In other words, the technology of hypertext brings something new into the world, something that we could not have imagined on our own.

Such sentiments carry through into the second strand in which hypertext is positioned in relation to modern and postmodern literature. What is significant here is the concept of the avant-garde, which in the case of creative work signifies writers, artists and intellectuals who were literally ahead of their time and, as a result, often misunderstood or unappreciated. Again, the discursive bias here is toward one of progress and, more specifically, toward a vision of the future that values experimentation, the rejection of tradition and free, unhindered expression. As such, hypertext becomes a technologized embodiment of the avant-garde, dedicated, as Eastgate Systems reminds us, to "serious" intellectual and creative work. The Eastgate Systems slogan is doubly interesting in that it reaffirms high modernism's dismissal of the "less serious" accomplishments of popular and commercial culture—an attitude typified by one of modernism's greatest champions, Theodor Adorno. Of course many of the individual works in Eastgate's catalog are typically postmodern in the sense that many aspects of popular culture are integrated into the individual works. However, what can still be maintained is that the more "respected" manifestations of creative work in hypertext or hypermedia is distanced from popular culture in general and mainstream Web-based hypertext in particular.

The historical legacies of the various pioneers each in their own way resonate with a technical code that is built around the assumption of technology as an evolutionary force that is capable of leading humanity into new and in some cases necessary directions. Consider once again the grandfather of hypertext Vannevar Bush and his vision of the memex as being an "intimate supplement" to memory by which the thought patterns and characteristics of a particular user can be preserved for future generations. Think also of Bush's impatience with the data management techniques of his time and his concern that human beings were losing their ability to manage their own information spaces at an alarming and increasing rate. The imaginary memex thus represents an important way out of this perceived morass as well as serves as an inspirational mythical object that continues to inspire developers to this day. Douglas Engelbart and Ted Nelson are also men driven by a desire to create technologies that will allow us to transcend current limits and, in Engelbart's case, to actually augment or enhance ourselves in a fundamental way. Nelson's aims are driven by a fervent desire to revolutionize society as a whole via a network of "freedom machines" that would bring about an almost utopian society of free exchange and unbounded creative expression.

Such revolutionary goals, while considerably muted and perhaps more informed by practical agendas, are also evident in the various software platforms discussed in this chapter. Equally pioneering in their aim to create usable hypertext systems, programs such as Intermedia and Storyspace are important historical markers because of their ability to materially realize alternate paradigms for writing and expression in general. The concept of paradigms is an important one and will in fact serve as a means to bring this chapter to a close. Briefly stated, a paradigm is a shared set of assumptions, concepts and values that are integral to how a community views and understands reality. In the case of hypertext, what is significant here is the manner in which it is being described and employed as a general paradigm with which to define and structure the very nature of expression itself, especially in terms of the relationships between readers and writers. Hypertext systems, such as Intermedia, are thus not only seductive tools but also materialized principles that effectively realize a set of principles, visions and beliefs, or even, to take a term from Heidegger, a way of "being." Like all forms of technology, hypertext has an immediate and intimate social dimension that essentially means that it is a part of our lifeworld and, in fact, is often inseparable from how we live and experience what we understand as reality. Indeed, as Vivian Sobchack notes, different technologies offer our "lived bodies" different ways of being in the world and as such have the potential to alter our very identity. A key element here is the manner in which technologies of representation affect our sense of time, space and existential embodied presence.

Sobchack claims that "cinematic and electronic technologies have transformed us so that we presently see, sense and make sense of ourselves in different ways."[51] In the case of cinema, the technology actually replicates our experience of objective, embodied vision, meaning that it reflects our understanding of what it means to see with our natural eyes. In other words, the movie camera is like an eye in so much that it observes the world in a way that is analogous to how we observe it as well. Electronic technology, on the other hand, is very different in that it is completely disembodied and "bound up in a centerless, network like structure of instant stimulation and desire." As a result, electronic spaces are "phenomenologically experienced as simultaneous, disperse and insubstantial," meaning that, for Sobchack at least, electronic presence cannot be experienced or understood with direct analogs or comparisons to lived, embodied experience. On the net or within the mazes of cyberspace, we effectively lose our bodies insomuch that our identities and the way in which we represent ourselves (and experience the representations of others) is no longer tied to bodily experience or even reference.

How do such lofty and abstract ideas apply to the history of hypertext? My basic argument here is that the history of the hypertext medium reveals a bias toward a literal "virtualization" of the experience of representation. Although often employing spatial metaphors, as in the case of programs such as Storyspace or even HyperCard, the actual experience of writing and reading hypertext (or hypermedia) is represented as one that takes place within a different place—a place in which conventional relationships are shifted and redefined, a place where, to quote the hypermedia artist Mark Amerika, writing becomes "a hybridized art practice that performs with and in the networked space of flows," a place where mind, body and machine merge, a place where progress and evolution are enacted and championed and a place where a bright future of interactive sharing and expression can be finally realized.[52] So while the history of hypertext, as represented in this chapter, is made up of a diverse cast of characters, devices and visions, a common discursive trajectory can be identified. Such an identification is important in terms of helping us understand that hypertext, like any technology, is not just a neutral and technical application of knowledge. Rather, hypertext speaks to its origins in terms of manifesting very particular dreams, visions and biases. Thus, in order to appreciate its wider significance, it is important to listen to the messages that lie behind the smooth interfaces of the machine.

Further Reading

Barret, E. Ed. *Text, ConText and HyperText. Writing with and for the Computer.* Cambridge and London: MIT Press, 1988.

Berk, E. and J. Devlin. Eds. *Hypertext/Hypermedia Handbook.* New York: McGraw-Hill, 1991.

Birkerts, Sven. *Gutenberg Elegies: The Fate of Reading in an Electronic Age.* Boston: Faber and Faber, 1994.

Englebart, Douglas et al. (1970). Collected articles and unpublished papers. Freemont CA: Bootstrap Institute. http://www.bootstrap.org/institute/bibliography.html

chapter **2**

Hypertext in Use

It is tempting, especially in books such as this, to represent hypertext with a single brushstroke. Although perhaps efficient in terms of providing a general idea of hypertext's major properties and applications, such a tactic does not fully capture the diversity of the medium nor adequately acknowledge the sheer inventiveness of the many developers, writers and artists working with hypermedia in all its forms. Thus, the major aim of this chapter is to map out a survey of common uses and normative practices so that readers can gain a broad understanding of the major conventions, genres and directions of hypertext. Such an understanding is necessary in order to pursue more detailed work on the medium as well as to gain an informed appreciation of hypertext's unique and potentially transformative characteristics.

Hardly all encompassing, hypertext and hypermedia practice can be broadly grouped into the following (and not mutually exclusive) categories:

1. Hypertext on the shelf—literary and artistic hypertext and hypermedia.
2. Hypertext in the classroom—educational uses of hypertext and hypermedia.
3. Hypertext at work—informational uses of hypertext technology.
4. Hypertext at play—uses of hypertext as a general platform for game play.

Hypertext on the Shelf

The use of hypertext for purely creative purposes, such as in the creation of fiction or poetry, is in some ways the most compelling and at the same time confusing uses of the medium. As discussed in Chapter 1, many of the literary approaches to hypertext take their cues from modern and postmodern experimental literature. While this is indeed a major aspect of literary hypertext (or hyperfiction), it is by no means the only approach. However, in the majority of books and articles that discusses the merits of hypertext in terms of it being an important innovation in how "serious" writers approach their craft, it is these hyperfictions that gain the bulk of critical attention. For many, it was Robert Coover's review and article for the *New York Times* that first brought hyperfiction to the general public and, for that matter, to many academics. Published in June 1992, Coover's text enthusiastically embraces hypertext as a "truly new and unique environment," detailing his various encounters with the now classic works of hyperfiction and his experience of teaching creative writing using Intermedia and Storyspace. Coover himself, it should be noted, is a well-known author and champion of experimental fiction and has published over fourteen books, his latest being *Whatever Happened to Gloomy Gus of the Chicago Bears*, which explores the life of another Richard Nixon—a Nixon who instead of entering politics became obsessed with football and sex. In addition to his writing, Coover is well known as an innovative teacher of creative writing who has, in fact, actively embraced the use of hypertext in his classrooms.

The majority of literary hypertexts that has received any sustained attention from academics and critics tend to be published through Eastgate Systems, which is perhaps not all that surprising given that the company offers one of the few remaining authoring systems dedicated to the creation of "serious hypertexts." In addition, the company is a decisive champion for authors, both new and established, who wish to explore the potentials of electronic fiction, nonfiction and poetry. Browsing through the Eastgate catalog does indeed give the impression that hypertext writing is a "serious" affair given that the range of topics, subject matter, approaches and styles are both diverse and well developed. Though much of the fiction and poetry is decidedly "experimental" in the sense of going beyond the traditional conventions of linear narrative and genre, they cannot be characterized as adhering to a common style or approach with the exception perhaps of their common use of Storyspace. In other words, the hypernovels, poems and nonfiction works published by Eastgate are as unique as the authors who write them. While this may seem like a rather obvious and unremarkable point, it remains important for the simple reason that it is again tempting to embrace or dismiss literary hypertext as a tangled web of associations, fleeting references and narrative strands that keep narrative closure forever at bay. If literary hypertext has anything in common, it is, as J. Yellowlees Douglas notes, its tendency to follow the paths of late twentieth-century fiction "characterized by multiple perspectives and voices, episodes linked with associative logic and memory, and rejection of conventional, often pat, final awarding of marriages, happiness, money, and recognition that wrap up narratives in mainstream and genre fiction alike."[1] Many authors are also united by a shared desire to explore the nature of electronic writing in the sense of exploring what the technology can and cannot do in terms of presenting compelling and meaningful creative work.

Eastgate Systems, despite its relative ubiquity in the world of literary hypertext, is not the only game in the town called hypertext. Though it is basically the only publishing company specifically dedicated to hypertext, many important and creative works are being published on the World Wide Web. Once again, the range of approaches, aesthetics and levels of quality are diverse and difficult to classify and, as such, it is impossible to offer anything even close to a comprehensive overview of what is currently available. However, as a means to offer some measure of guidance, it is possible to construct a crude and very general classification system as a means to group literary hypertexts into a number of manageable categories.

1. Completely text-based conventional hypertexts.
2. Hypermedia sites that incorporate visuals and sounds as supplements to textual content.
3. Dynamic hypermedia sites where text has given way to a primarily visual aesthetic.

Text-Based Hypertexts

The first category could be considered the "classic mode" in so much that the initial forays of hypertext were almost entirely text based that can be attributed mainly, but not exclusively, to the limits of early hypertext technology and display terminals. That said, the exclusivity of text is not only a matter of constraint but also of conscious choice on the part of writers. It is important to remember that hypertext technology, such as HyperCard or Storyspace, is considered by many as a new medium for *writers* and *readers* and is therefore primarily a medium with which to experiment with the written word itself. Images and sound effects are merely window dressing. What counts are the words.

Such a sentiment is certainly emphasized by Robert Coover who, in his keynote address for the 1999 Digital Arts and Culture Conference in Atlanta, Georgia, mourned the passing of what he termed the "Golden Age of Hypertext"—an age where pioneering hypertext writers "explored the tantalizing new possibility of laying a story out spatially instead of linearly, inviting the reader to explore it as one might explore one's memory or wander a many-pathed geographical terrain, and, being adventurous quests at the edge of a new literary frontier, they were often intensely self-reflective."[2] With the advent of the World Wide Web and multimedia computing, such noble pursuits have given way to meaningless "image surfing" where the art of letters loses its substance and becomes reduced to "surface spectacle." Coover is no doubt overstating his disdain for media-rich hypertexts in an effort to point out what he believes to have been truly revolutionary about hypertext, namely the manner in which it served as a platform for radical experiments with the written word. In his commentary on Shelley Jackson's *Patchwork Girl*, Coover reminisces over what he feels was truly remarkable about so-called classic hyperfiction:

> These early multidirectional webworks of text spaces had the alleged disadvantage—a disadvantage that has all but disappeared—of having to click a mouse and read from a screen, relatively new experiences then, but they challenged the constraints and conventions of centuries of printbound reading in very exciting ways, offering the writer vast new formal possibilities and redefining the relationship of the reader to the text.

Coover could be accused of being overly nostalgic over this apparent "Golden Age" which is something he readily acknowledges within the course of his address. Indeed, there is much to take issue with regard to Coover's negative assessment of hypertext that integrates visual and audio material—an issue that will be explored in greater depth Chapter 3. For now, what is noteworthy of Coover's emphasis on classic hyperfiction is simply the fact that such works compel us to focus on what hypertext means in terms of reading and writing. Such a focus is crucial given that it serves as a basis for much of the theoretical and creative work within the domain of digital media as a whole.

A fairly recent example of a hypertext novel that keeps to Coover's classic ideal is Judy Malloy's 2004 Web fiction *Revelations of Secret Surveillance*, a Web-based hyperfiction that concerns the difficulties that artists in the United States face in an age of "covert surveillance and harassment" by US intelligence agencies.[3] Aside from a simple low-resolution front page, Malloy's work is entirely text based and employs an interface that is almost retro given its simplicity and unadorned design. She composed the work using "Narrabase," a database strategy that she created in 1986. In her words, Narrabase "uses a computer database as a way to build up levels of meaning and to show many aspects of the story and characters, rather than as a means of providing alternative plot turns and endings."[4] The experience of reading such a work is akin to repeatedly plunging into a pool of information from which a reader would emerge with "a cumulative and individual picture."[5]

In an age where design is king, Malloy's hypertext novel is not that much to look at and, as such, certainly goes against general aesthetic trends in Web design. The first page features a simple black box within which, written in white, is the first "scene" of the novel. Around this block of text are arranged (against a rather acidic green background) a series of chapter titles and phrases that serve as links. The reader can go through the work by either clicking on these links or by

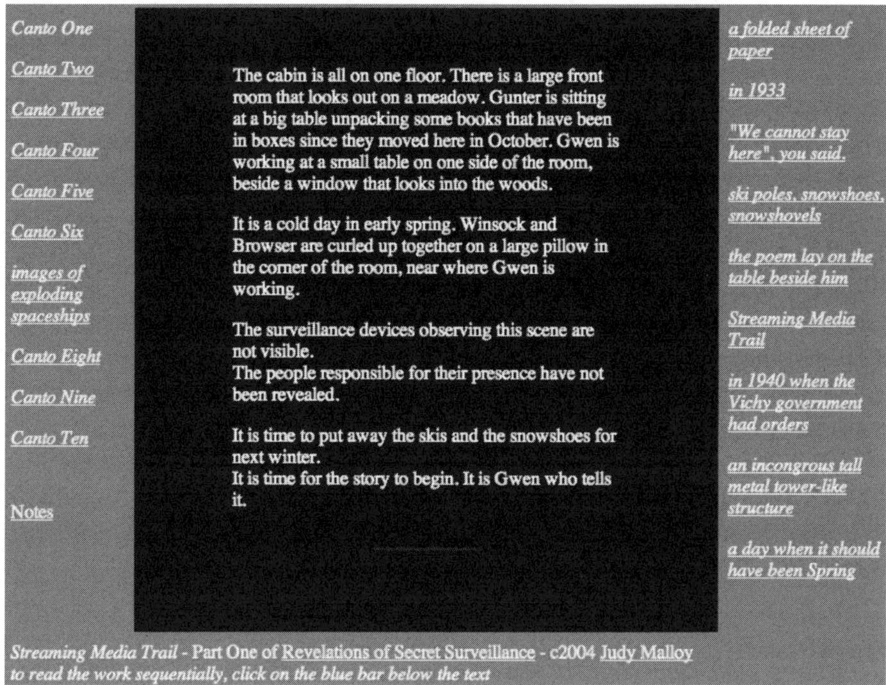

Figure 4. Screenshot from "Canto One" of *Revelations* by Judy Malloy.

reading the work sequentially by way of the "blue bar" at the bottom of the page. The links on the right hand of the page take the reader to various points within a particular "canto" whereas the links on the left allow the reader to traverse the ten major sections of the novel as a whole (Figure 4). As the reader clicks on a link on the right, the text in the center changes and an additional link is added to the list on the bottom. Eventually the links begin to repeat themselves and at that point the reader can move on to the next "canto."

The narrative structure of *Revelations* is relatively conventional in that it follows the familiar pattern of alternating between the memories of the main characters, in this case Gwen and her memories of how she met her husband Gunter in Germany and the stories and recollections of Gunter's parents who were forced to flee Nazi Germany. In between such reflections is an additional narrative strand that concerns the life of the two main characters and their friends as they spend part of the winter in a New Hampshire cottage. Thematically, the novel draws parallels between the censorship and persecution of artists in Nazi Germany and the increasingly restrictive conditions for artists in post-9/11 America. Given the relatively simple structure of the interface (and also the option of the "blue bar"), Malloy's novel is a rather straightforward reading experience in the sense of not overwhelming

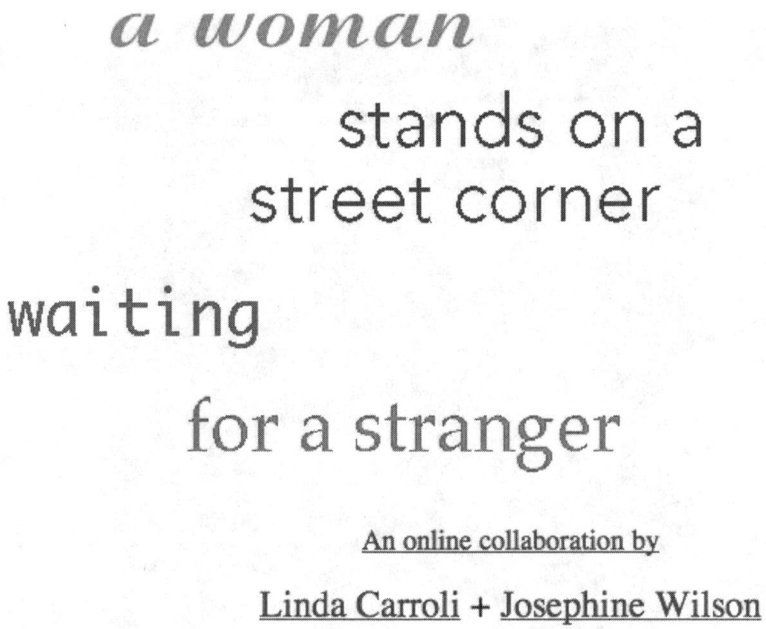

a woman

stands on a
street corner

waiting

for a stranger

An online collaboration by

Linda Carroli + Josephine Wilson

Figure 5. Screenshot of title page of *Water Writes Always in Plural.*

the reader with a multitude of links or fragmented narrative strands. Indeed, one might question whether the novel would work just as well as a conventional book given the comparatively 'linear' organization of the hypertext structure. Nevertheless, *Revelations* remains a satisfying experience due to the fact that the various narrative sequences, which are compelling in their own right, are not overshadowed by an overly complex interface and linking structure.

Simple Hypermedia

In the second instance, the collaborative work *Water Writes Always in Plural* (*WWAP*) by Linda Carroli and Josephine Wilson is characteristic of works that privilege an aesthetic of textual links and incorporate sounds or visuals mainly to supplement the textual content. WWAP was funded by the New Media Arts Fund of the Australia Council and received a number of awards, including the Salt Hill Award for Hypertext in 1999 and an honorary mention for the "Trace/AltX International Hypertext Award."[6] The opening of WWAP features a very simple arrangement of words and as is common for many hyperfictions offers little in the way of user instructions. However, given most people's familiarity with how Web pages work, the reader's first impulse will be to click on the words to see whether they are active links (Figure 5). Clicking on the first link, "a woman," leads to a page that offers a passage that is a blend of fictional and critical prose, with citations from the likes of Derrida and Cixous. "Can you wait for a completely empty signifier?" is a question asked near the beginning of the page.

As one moves through the text, it is clear that the authors intended the reader to question the very nature of the narrative and the conventions around which the character, plot and representation are constructed. "As writers/readers, we are in a dialogue through which we write the space between as a desiring narrative." Clicking on the remaining texts also produces a similar introductory sequence where normative hypertext paradigms and catchwords are dispersed—labyrinths, the I Ching, forking paths, threads, uncertainty, chance, pathways and the unexpected. What is particularly intriguing about WWAP is the speed at which it forces readers to make connections between their own wait for the text to begin and the plot device of a woman waiting for a "stranger" on a street corner to move the narrative (and her fate) along. As the authors ironically state, "And that, dear scrollers, is surely the definition of a story. So what the hell is all that complaining about?"

As one moves through and past the introductory sections, one comes very quickly into familiar hypertext territory. The number of links is kept to a manageable level and in many cases readers have only one or two choices within a given passage. In many cases, the choices that readers make render circular patterns of repetition, given that all but one pathway leads back to the beginning passage "a woman stands on a street corner waiting for a stranger." The only trail of links that does not lead back to the beginning is a sequence that concerns a woman who is waiting for a "white knight" to come and rescue her. Unlike all the other paths, this one leads to a literal dead end, depicting a triumphant soldier sitting on a white stallion with the caption "he will rescue her." Aside from this image, the only text is the statement "go back. This is a dead end." What can be inferred from this sequence is of course that the conventional happy ending where the prince or hero arrives just in time is not one that will lead us anywhere interesting. Such a sentiment applies as much to the art of narrative as it does to conventional gender relationships. Action or agency is thus preferable to passive waiting.

Though mainly ancillary to the textual content, the images and sounds add an intriguing element to the experience of WWAP by heightening certain moods or by adding an extra level of meaning. Within one of the lexias, the text of a school song is displayed while the tune of "It's a Small World After All," rendered on a creaky music box, plays in the background. The effect is a somewhat unsettling blend of nostalgia and naive charm that enriches rather than distracts the reader from the textual content. A similar effect is achieved in the lexia "what is a foreigner" that probes the meaning and experience of being a stranger and a designated other. Playing in the background is the telephone voice menu from Australia's Department of Immigration and Multicultural Affairs Information

Line, which features a ubiquitous female voice offering a range of options, accessible from the telephone's key pad. The voice moves through a range of common immigration and residency options ending with the "if you are in Australia and want to seek Australia's protection as a refugee, please press one." At this point a loop begins with the sound of a key being depressed and another older voice stating "this is not a valid mail box number," and the refugee option playing over and over again. The effect of this sequence plays on the experience that most of us have had with such automated services—frustration, disempowerment and utter voicelessness—but with the added context of what this might mean for a new immigrant.

WWAP, though technically quite simple, is one of the more compelling examples of hyperfiction and a representative of works that employ audiovisual elements as support material for text-based narrative. As in the previous category of exclusively text-based works, success is contingent on good writing—something that can be said of WWAP. Each of the individual lexias and pages is an evocative blend of narrative threads and critical musings that are meaningful in and of themselves. Links are kept to a minimum, sometimes only one to a page and, for the most part, have an obvious and direct relationship to the texts to which they are connected. One effect is that the reading experience is not one of immediate confusion and displacement—a common complaint among those encountering literary hypertext for the first time. Of course, this is not to say that the success of a given hypertext is contingent upon keeping links to a minimum as there are certainly many works that are much more complex and dense than WWAP and equally effective in terms of being engaging and compelling. Like any other art form, there is no recipe for literary hypertext.

Dynamic Hypermedia

The third category of literary hypertexts is made up of works that often stray very far from the written word and employ techniques and aesthetics taken from cinema, advertising and television, to name only a few influences. One characteristic example is the enigmatic and often confounding *Filmtext*, created by Mark Amerika, a well-known writer and theorist of hypermedia. Even after repeated visits, it is difficult to say what exactly *Filmtext* is. Amerika's work seems to have a life of its own and, as such, refuses many of the conventions that define the nature and experience of narrative. *Filmtext* is actually part of a "Net art trilogy" that includes *Grammatron* (1993–1997) and *Phon:E:Me* (1999) that, in Amerika's words, attempts "to show how writing is becoming more performative in a network-distributed environment."

> In all these digital artworks, I approach computer-mediated network environment of the World Wide Web as an experiential writing zone, one where the evolving language of new

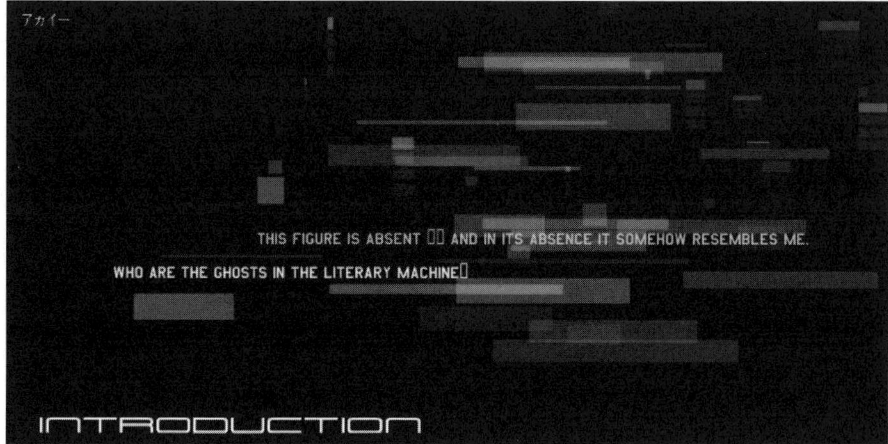

Figure 6. Introduction to *Filmtext 2.0*.

> media would reflect the convergence of image-writing, sound-writing, language-writing and code-writing as complementary processes that would feed off each other and, in so doing, contributed to the construction of interactive digital narratives programmed to challenge the way we compose, exhibit and distribute art in network culture.[7]

The effect of such converging processes is, as stated above, difficult to classify. Upon opening *Filmtext*, we are greeted by an "introduction," which consists of an animated sequence of words, disrupted grid patterns and what appears to be Japanese characters. In the background rumbles a disjointed, electroindustrial soundtrack (Figure 6).[8]

Instructions about how to navigate the site are kept to a bare minimum. The menu consists of a series of pseudo-Japanese symbols which when accessed take the reader through the various levels of *Filmtext*. However, it is possible to also do nothing at this introductory stage and simply let the animation sequence run its course which takes about three minutes. At that point, a small menu appears with the message "authorized for next level." Clicking on the icon renders a new screen—a desolate, otherworldly landscape of what appears to be extinct volcanoes (Figure 7).

Again, the user interface is enigmatic. Moving the mouse over the mouths of any one of the volcanoes causes a light beam to emerge, and after a few seconds, a secondary screen appears that triggers a sequence of code like text, a number of video animations and various audio samples that the reader can turn on or off to create a layered soundtrack of sorts (Figure 8). And so it continues.

As one moves through the various stages, a similar mechanism of user-initiated hotspots renders video loops, a mixture of computer code and theoretical

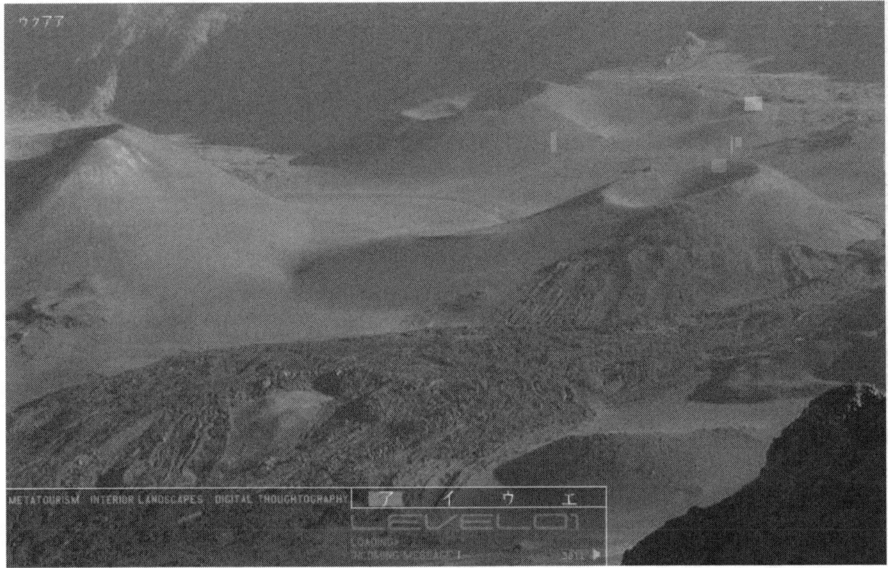

Figure 7. Level One of *Filmtext 2.0*.

reflections, audio samples and animations. The pressing question, of course, is what is *Filmtext* about? Some of the text within the Web site offers a few clues:

> Circulating within a network, hotly pursuing a nomadic journey to the end of the night.
>
> But the journey to the end of the night does not reach its much-vaunted conclusion (imaginary endgame) at the light of day...
>
> A command-and-control storyworld camouflaged as a cluster of interconnected alien lightforms transmitting simultaneous explosions of well-rehearsed action scripts writing out a psychosynaesthetic language in mercurial QuickTime.

What is suggested here is that the experience of *Filmtext* is to a significant degree what *Filmtext* is "about" and that its meaning is not so much contained within the content but rather via the actions, experiences and impressions of individual readers. "Interacting with the site," states Amerika, "requires the visitor to become a viewer, a reader, a DJ/VJ, an art appreciator, a network navigator and an interactive participant who can—working within the parameters set by the artist—create her or his own ambient game environment, electronic literary experience and digitally expanded cinema, all at the same time."[9]

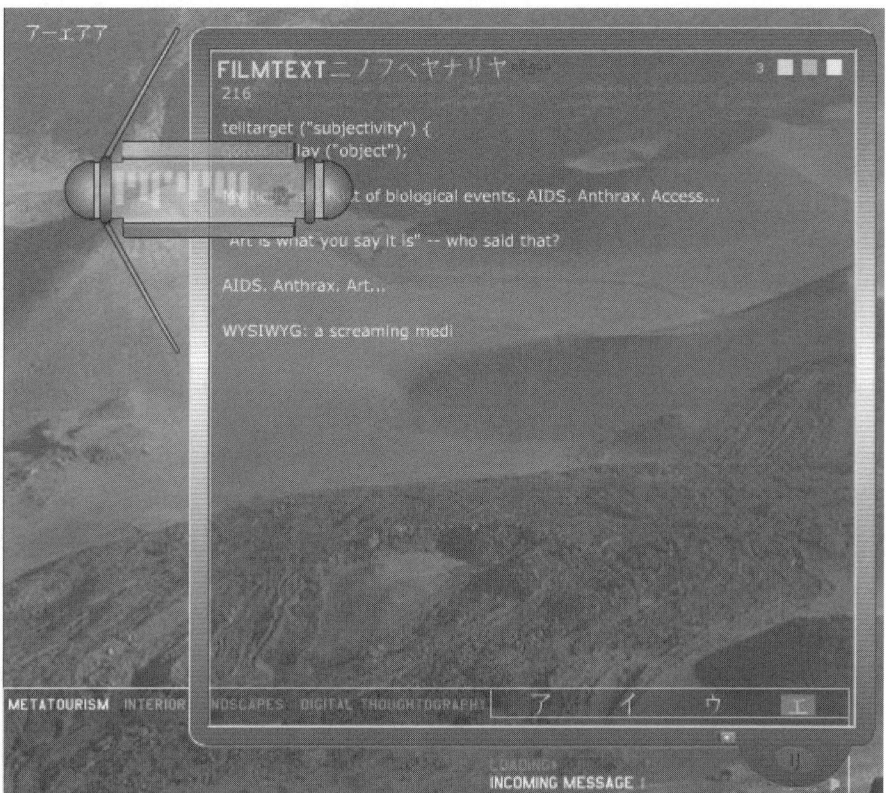

Figure 8. Popup animation, Level One of *Filmtext 2.0*.

Clearly, we are a long way from the written word and the conventions of print culture and have entered into a world of hybrid forms that challenge just about everything to do with narrative, representation and meaning. The effects are ultimately mixed. On the one hand, *Filmtext* is an intriguing and elaborate theoretical exercise that materializes many of the theoretical concepts around hypermedia (which will be discussed in Chapter 3). On the other hand, the work tends to overstate its theoretical inventions and thus effectively hits the user on the head with a theoretical hammer over and over again. While visually and aurally interesting at first, the various devices and sequences begin to wane as they become familiar. After some time, the pseudotheoretical code text all begins to look all the same, as do the various video sequences, leaving the reader (at least this one) increasingly restless and even bored. That said, *Filmtext*, and Amerika's work in general, does make an important and notable contribution to digital media art and offers a visceral meditation on the effects of digital media on the present and future of narrative and representation.

Hypertext in the Classroom

Given the claims that hypertext has the potential to radically alter the conventions of reading and writing (for better or worse), it should be of no surprise that hypertext has also been touted as being a revolutionary force within the world of education. Central to its impact is the manner in which it is said to put "students in charge of their learning, making knowledge more accessible, encouraging creativity, and adding excitement and fun to education."[10] As a decentralized, nonlinear system, hypertext, at least as envisioned by Ted Nelson, provides a powerful alternative to the traditional modes of learning in which an authoritarian teacher merely delivers content to a group of passive students. Instead, with hypertext, students are motivated by the system to form a dynamic two-way relationship with the subject matter in which progress through the material is motivated by their own interests and pathways:

> At no previous time has it been possible to create learning resources so responsive and interesting, or to give such free play to the student's initiative as we may now. We can now build computer-based presentational wonderlands, where a student (or other user) may browse and ramble through a vast variety of writings, pictures and apparitions in magical space, as well as rich data structures and facilities for twiddling them.[11]

Behind Nelson's enthusiastic musings lie a host of complex issues and questions not the least of which is the matter of how best to define and conceptualize education and, moreover, the challenge of accurately assessing the effects of a given pedagogical system. The primary focus of this section is on the explicit use of hypertext technology in an educational setting and not on the much larger category of computer-assisted learning that includes the vast area of distance education. Of course both Computer Aided Learning (CAL) and distance-ed may or may not incorporate hypertext within their various platforms or approaches. However, the point I want make is simply that the use of a computer in a learning situation does not necessarily involve hypertext as either a paradigm or an application.

That said, what are some of the typical aims and promises of a hypertext-based pedagogical system? For the sake of brevity, here is yet another list:

1. To encourage self-directed and self-motivated learning habits or "hyperlearning."
2. To reconfigure the traditional roles of teachers and students into a more cooperative and interactive relationship.
3. To individualize the learning experience.
4. To craft the art of connection: for a hypertext learner and teacher, everything is potentially connected.

5. To develop critical skills and habits of thinking based on multiplicity.
6. To empower students (and one would hope teachers) by "placing them inside rather than outside the world of research and scholarly debate."[12]
7. To encourage collaborative learning and "take advantage of distributed expertise by the community."[13]
8. To use computer technology as a means to create an individualized knowledge base, much in the spirit of Vannevar Bush's memex.
9. To make information and knowledge accessible over a network rather than via brick-and-mortar institutions.
10. To encourage and facilitate a community-oriented approach to learning and teaching.

"Net Frog": Procedural Hyperlearning

How are such goals achieved? As one might suspect, there is no one ideal approach or system, and hypertext developers are still exploring (and some might be struggling with) new methods and platforms. At the heart of most systems, including such important benchmarks as Intermedia, are interfaces that encourage students to actively explore a given topic by way of engaging in a number of activities and learning pathways that have some measure of self-direction. One typical example in which students learn a combination of theoretical and practical skills is "Net Frog—The On-Line Dissection," created by Mable Kinzie at the University of Virginia's Curry School of Education.[14] The site allows high school students to learn about the steps involved in the successful dissection of a frog while learning about its various organs, and also its relationship to other animals, including humans. The interface is relatively simple and also offers an internal reference dictionary where highlighted words are defined and explained, audio and video documentation of an actual dissection, a link for additional information and a diagnostic quiz to test the students' comprehension of the material (Figure 9).

The "virtual dissection" option is made available via a simple "point-and-click" mechanisms by which students are requested to identify the correct places to pin the frog or make the first incision. Clicking on the correct area elicits a positive response whereas a wrong choice prompts students to "try again" (and again and again until they get it right). Although rather mechanical and procedural, "Net Frog," has quite a number of core hypertextual elements such as allowing students to choose from a limited range of options to enhance their learning experience and the ability to proceed through the material at their own pace. The video and audio elements serve to enhance further and illustrate the material whereas the diagnostic quiz offers a minimal form of feedback from the system. The rather

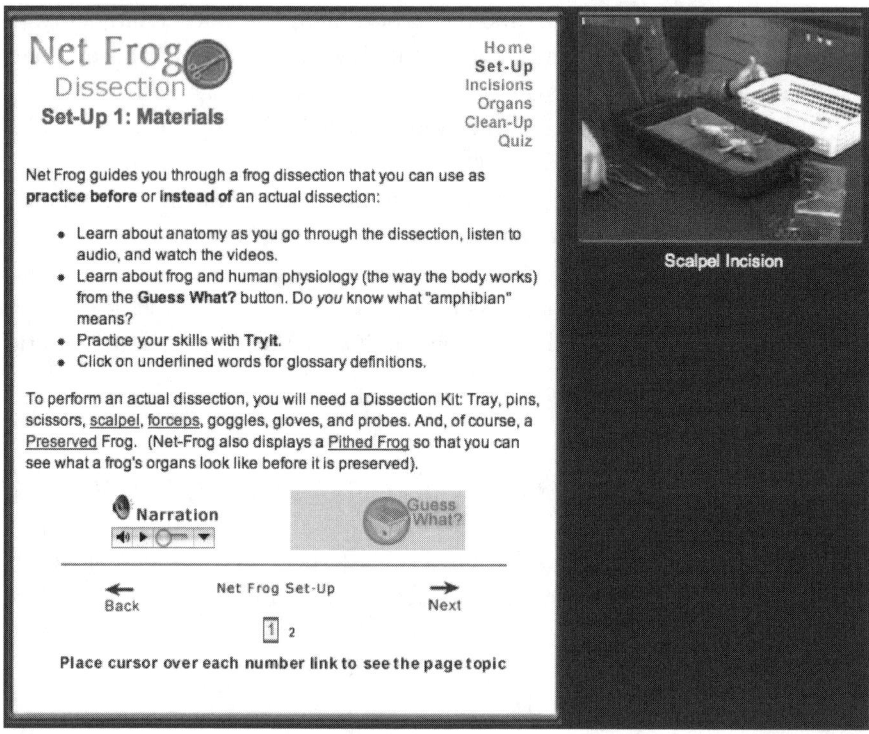

Figure 9. Set-up menu and instructions in "Net Frog."

primitive virtual dissection interface allows for a rudimentary interactive experience where students, at the very least, are provided with a visual map of the major steps of the dissection.

To appreciate the value of "Net Frog," which is just one of many similar virtual dissection and surgery tools currently on the market, traditional books offer a notable point of comparison. Obviously a book can neither offer the same level of interactivity nor can it incorporate visual and audio examples to the same degree as a digital application. The "do-it-yourself" quality that "Net Frog" offers is also not possible in print. Compared to an actual dissection, "Net Frog" is not a complete substitute, although studies show that students who participate in virtual dissections fare just as well as, if not better than, those who learn through more conventional laboratory-based work.[15]

Hypertext and New Forms of Learning

While innovative and effective in their own rights, applications such as "Net Frog" are relatively simple uses of the hypertext paradigm insomuch that their educational goals are confined to a set of concrete skills and a particular base of knowledge from which to exercise those skills. The program also limits the interactive and hypertextual components to interactions within the system itself, such as in the form of diagnostic quizzes or the "virtual dissection" mechanism. However, matters become decidedly more complex and arguably more in line with the full potential of hypertext the moment that hypertext is used to alter the conventional structures and dynamics of formal education itself rather than serving as a supplement to already existing systems. Among the pioneers of hypertext-based education is Brown University that hosted some of the first completely computer-based courses with George Landow leading the development in several courses in English Literature, notably the "In Memoriam Web," a study of Tennyson's poem and the "Dickens Web," the latter of which can now be purchased through Eastgate Systems. In writing about his and other courses, Landow identifies three major qualities of hypertext that are valuable for both students and faculty—connectivity, preservation and accessibility. In the first instance, what Landow, among others, values about hypertext as an educational resource is its ability to foster a strong sense and material base for collaboration and community. Landow argues that "the essential connectivity of hypertext encourages and demands collaboration. By making each document in the docuverse exist as part of a larger structure, hypertext places each document in what one can term the 'virtual presence' of all previously created documents and their creators."[16] While such a collaborative environment can certainly exist within a brick and mortar classroom, research and field experience seems to indicate that hypertext enhances the cooperative spirit of students and teachers.

For Landow there are four major ways in which a student enters into a collaborate relationship with a hypertext-based course.[17] The first is the seemingly simple act of reading the course content, which in the case of hypertext means that the "reading path" is shaped by individual students who follow links according to their own interests and needs. Second, students can create links between and within the documents made available through the hypertext courseware. The third and fourth types of collaboration involve the ability to create files, either text or audio/visual, that can be linked to the hypertext system. To this list can be added the possibility of various other forms of collaborative devices, such as online, real-time discussion forums or chats, student and teacher Web-logs ("blogs"), online editing tools for peer reviews and other such devices.

Preservation, the second major quality of hypertext that Landow identifies describes the manner in which a given "hypertext corpus" serves as an efficient and dynamic reservoir of past work that can be continually updated and reorganized for a variety of purposes. Such a quality is of great importance for instructors who could use the flexibility of a hypertext system to create new courses, update existing courses or make connections between their courses and that of others as a means to broaden and conceptualize particular topics. "[S]omeone teaching an English course that concentrates on literary technique of the nineteenth-century novel can nonetheless draw upon relevant materials in political, social, urban, technological, and religious history. All of us try to allude to such aspects of context, but the limitations of time and the need to cover the central concerns of the course often leave students with a decontextualized, distorted view."[18] As Landow points out, what he describes resembles Bush's dream of creating an "intimate supplement" to memory or the mind that parallels the flexibility and adaptability of human ability to constantly absorb and reconfigure both new and existing knowledge for an infinite number of uses. In this way, the hypertext system created by Professor Smith becomes more than just a container for information and lecture notes but rather a mutable and almost organic companion that can continually evolve as "Prof. Smith" moves through his career and develops new interests.

The final hypertext quality, accessibility, refers to the fact that hypertext and the computer in general allow both students and teachers to engage in a course with a much greater degree of freedom and flexibility than conventional courses that meet in a particular place and at a particular time. This, of course, is also the big draw with distance education that allows for a far greater degree of access to students in remote areas or to students (and faculty) who might find it difficult to meet in a physical location at a specified time. In addition, students and teachers can also take advantage of a host of additional tools, such as external databases, communication tools (such as chats) and material archived within the course's network. Finally, a computer-based education system, whether utilizing hypertext or not, also has the potential to overcome obstacles that often complicate the dynamics of "flesh-and-blood" classrooms, for example, shy students who may be uncomfortable about speaking in public or the difficulties involved in organizing discussions for very large numbers of students.[19]

In terms of specific examples and uses of hypertext in an educational setting, the majority of documented cases dates from the mid-1980s to the very tail end of the twentieth century. Indeed, most literature on educational hypertext details the use of programs that no longer exist, notably HyperCard, Intermedia, Guide and Hyperties. In many ways, the World Wide Web has replaced these and many other programs and now functions as the primary vehicle for delivering educational content electronically. For some, the Web's ubiquity is far from "the real dream" of hypertext first envisioned by Nelson and carried through in subsequent efforts. On the Xanadu Web site, Nelson (presumably) states that "today's popular software simulates paper. The World Wide Web (another imitation of paper) trivializes our original hypertext model with one-way ever-breaking links and no management of version or contents."[20] Such reservations are also shared by

Landow who comments that the Web lacks the "one to many linking"[21] and favors instead a "relatively flat version of hypertext" that relies too much on print media for its metaphorical base.[22] Mark Berstein, head of Eastgate Systems, notes that the Web lacks the types of dynamic links that can be found in other hypertext systems (such as Storyspace). Dynamic links are sensitive to where the reader has been before in a given document meaning that certain pathways can be blocked to readers who have or have not accessed specific links. Such "state-dependent behaviors" are difficult to create in conventional Web browsers and remain the exception rather than the rule.[23] Many of these limitations can be blamed on the nature of HTML (hypertext markup language), which is a "subprotocol" that "defines the internal structure of the Web's documents."[24] In his provocatively entitled article "The Inevitable Demise of the Web," Hal Berghel notes that the "Web is fundamentally egocentric. That is, from any user's perspective, the Web appears as a collection of resources locatable through a single link, or a link of that link, and so on. A Web 'database' is thus a stratified or flat collection with no superimposed structure" that is in marked contrast to the far more complex structures possible in programs such as Intermedia, Storyspace, Microcosm or Hyper-G.[25] In terms of the present discussion, what is important to note here is that while the World Wide Web currently dominates the educational uses of hypertext, it is by no means the "best way" in terms of fulfilling some of the theories and visions of "true hypertext."

Hypertext at Work

In many ways, hypertext has a central presence in most work environments, especially in the contemporary office space. Once again, this presence is manifested by the World Wide Web that many employees use as a means to reach customers, organize data and, to the dismay of some employers, to waste a bit of time. However, as should be apparent by now, there is more to hypertext than the Web which despite its ubiquity is considered a rather pared down version of the hypertext ideal.

While there is much more that could be explored in the context of this section, I concentrate on the use of hypertext technology to enhance or create collaboration within the workplace, especially around interpersonal communication and document creation. As a means to ground such a discussion, we can turn to the field of "computer supported cooperative work" (CSCW) and its closely related cousins of "workflow systems" and "groupware." CSCW grew out of a workshop organized by Iren Grief and Paul Cashman in 1984 to explore the role of technology in the work environment.[26] What specifically drove the CSCW pioneers was a desire to "learn more about how people work in groups and organizations and how technology affects that". Multidisciplinary by design, CSCW encompasses a range of approaches and research agendas that draw from the work of "economists, social psychologists, anthropologists, organizational theorists, educators, and anyone else who could shed light on group activity":

> People study, for example, the use, in group and organizational settings, of applications developed for individual users: the ways in which software developed to support groups, affects individuals and is adapted to different organizational contexts: and systems developed to support organizational goals as they act through individuals, groups, and projects.[27]

One of the chief strengths of hypertext is that it can function as a resource for collaborative work and as such has led to a number of experiments under the broad umbrella of CSCW. As part of the proceedings for Hypertext '91, a special panel was assembled to "discuss the relationship between hypertext as it is conceived and implemented today and requirements of current and future CSCW situations and applications."[28] Among the topics addressed was the extent to which nonlinearity and free association were necessary or even appropriate for cooperative work within or in conjunction with a computer-mediated environment. Hiroshi Ishii, of NTT Human Interface Labs in Japan, notes that nonlinearity provides a degree of flexibility when it comes to the expression and explorations of ideas; however, if left too unstructured, especially within the context of large groups or organizations, it could end up being counterproductive. Thomas Malone of MIT advocated a "semiformal" system that could incorporate the formal structures favored by computers and the informal methods preferred by humans. The advantage of a semiformal system is that it provides "a medium in which groups of people can develop, share and preserve shared understandings and group memories—and in which computational agents can help people find, filter, and process this shared knowledge."[29] A number of systems have been developed that offer the flexible and semiformal approach discussed by Malone and other like-minded researchers. Among these is the Cooperative Hypermedia Integrated with Process Support (CHIPS) developed by J.M. Haake and W. Wang in 1999. The system was developed to integrate "flexible business process modeling and execution capabilities into a collaborative hypermedia system." CHIPS is described as a "flexible hypertext system" that can accommodate "information structures in different degrees of formality."[30] In other words, CHIPS can work equally well with free-flowing associative representations of data as it can with highly rule-defined processes such as conventional databases. Such flexibility is possible through the use of "activity spaces" that utilize what is known as semantic networks. Semantic networks offer an alternative to the approach of most database management systems that "represent information in a simple record-based format," which are generally organized around clearly defined relationships and hierarchies.[31] In contrast, semantic networks allow for more complex data structures and encourage a "more navigational view of data relationships." A simpler way to put this is that semantic networks are schemes or systems that represent knowledge through nodes and links between nodes. The nodes are representative of concepts or objects and the links indicate the relationships between these nodes. As a simple example of a semantic net, think of a common word that is relatively rich in meaning such as the word "home." Now think of a few words that relate to "home," such as family or husband or front lawn or suburb. On a sheet of paper write down each of these words and draw a line linking them to the word home. Next, provide each line or link with a brief term that defines the relationship between the two words. If you continue this process, the network will gradually grow and the task of defining relationships between the words or nodes will become increasingly complex. Despite being overly simplistic, what should be clear from this example is that semantic networks offer a degree of flexibility and adaptability that rivals other more rigid forms of representing information.

Returning to CHIPS, the semantic network model is used to create a system of "activity spaces" that can be defined and structured according to the specific needs of the users and the type of information being represented and shared. The system actually incorporates three semantic dimensions: structural, relational and computational semantics. As is perhaps obvious from the terms themselves, the first dimension deals with the structure and constraints of a particular situation, the second describes the relationships between specific hypermedia objects and the third "describes the constraints, and triggering conditions attached to hypermedia objects."[32]

In their article describing the system, Haake and Wang provide a number of examples to illustrate how CHIPS could be used in a standard work situation. Among these is the rather familiar procedure of brainstorming where individuals meet, often at the very beginning of a new project, to present ideas in an unstructured and highly interactive fashion. For such a situation, a "white board" activity space would be defined in CHIPS that would be made available to all participants in real time. As on a real white board, the virtual version within CHIPS allows the participants to type, sketch, copy and paste directly into the activity space while engaging in either virtual or face-to-face informational communication. CHIPS can also facilitate co-decision making that requires a combination of formal relationships (following particular policies, for instance) and individually motivated and directed enquiries and agendas. For such a case, Haake and Wang "define three subtasks: initiating discussion, comparison and contrast and voting." The voting mechanism is highlighted in Figure 10, which exemplifies how CHIPS could be used to generate discussion and decision making around a particular issue, in this case, the question of whether to use the programming languages of Smalltalk or Java. As can be seen in the screenshot, the program allows

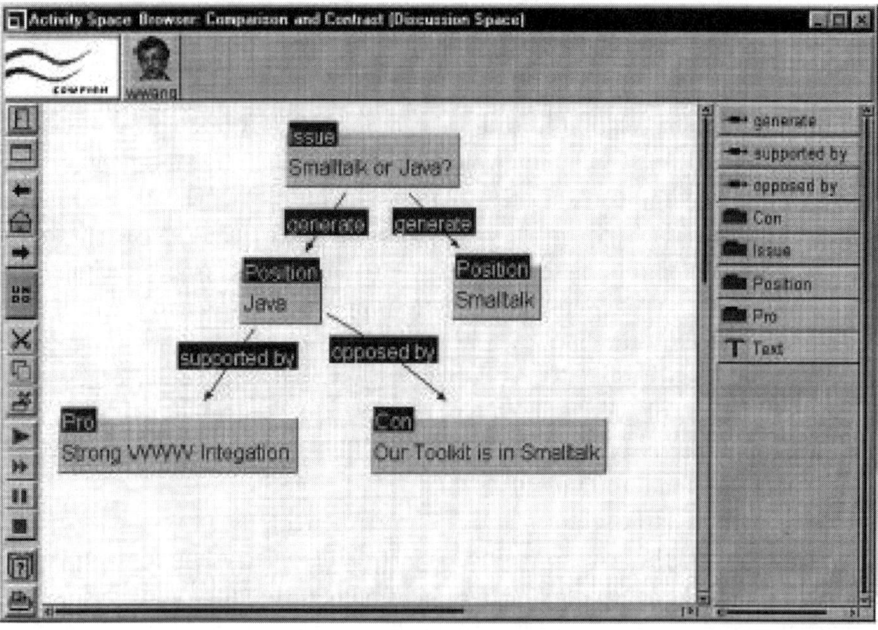

Figure 10. Voting system in CHIPS.

users to present opinions for or against each of the programming languages and to make such opinions available to anyone who is part of the project group. The "pro" and "con" boxes in the diagram are actually links that, when activated, reveal more detailed information regarding the specific positions. Once the team has had enough time to debate the issue, an internal and customizable voting program can be engaged to provide an overview of who is in favor of what.

Hypertext and Document Management

In many workplace settings, documents are often authored by more than one person. Here hypertext has been touted as a much-needed savior to what can potentially be a cumbersome and labor-intensive experience. A considerable amount of research has gone into the design of systems that can assist multiple authors, which in the case of business settings is frequently driven by the need to deliver fast and accurate results. An interesting example is provided by Timothy Miles-Board and Leslie Carr who created what they call "The Management Reporting System" or MRS. The system was designed to help mangers in the often complex and time-consuming process of producing management reports, which are often the cornerstones for an organization's information environment. Such reports are particularly challenging given that they are very much hybrid structures that rely on a web of existing and preexisting documents and notes:

> Management reporting is a complex, multistage activity which takes place in the context of other business processes and makes use of the multiple information systems that may have been provided for other purposes—general documentation, project management, financial control, email communication and business presentation. Managers treat information from these sources as "harvestable, contextualisable data," which is combined, summarized, and reinterpreted in management reports.[33]

Like many other scholars and developers, Miles-Board and Carr also note that the Web in its current incarnation is a rather limited tool as far as providing a dynamic and flexible authoring system is concerned and, in fact, has departed from the original conception and design of its inventor, Tim Berners-Lee. Today, the Web is very much a read-only system with very few mechanisms to allow casual users to personalize and adapt the Web pages they may browse.

Returning to the MRS, Miles-Board and Carr were driven to create a system that could bring together elements of open hypermedia, document creation and knowledge reuse in order to facilitate Web-based management reporting. In the first instance, open hypermedia refers to hypertexts "which are not confined to the boundaries of a single system, be it a Web browser, text editor, video streamer or midi player."[34]

The emphasis on document creation contrasts normative experience of the World Wide Web in so much that Web pages can usually be modified only by their creators or site administrators. The point of the MRS is that it opens up the Web as an all around writing/reading environment. The term "knowledge reuse" is meant to indicate a process more complex than the mere cutting and pasting of text from one document to another. The end result is a process that "assists managers by enabling new project summary reports to be written and delivered (fully linked) onto the Web for other managers to read and reuse."

There are essentially two major components of the MRS—the first being the "structure service" and the second the "document service." The structure service is responsible for taking care of the network, linking documents to one another and managing the multilevel references to documents in the document service. As one can assume from its title, the document service is the central place from where the management reports can be accessed. The service also ensures a level of standardization in terms of storing all documents in XML that allows them to be converted into either HTML or Microsoft Word. Furthermore, the service also provides several "templates" that can be used to produce new reports that correspond to the accepted standards and profiles of the company. The structure service stores and tracks the contributions, annotations and linking patterns of the IT managers reading and/or producing the reports. In essence, the MRS stores the annotations to and adaptations of existing or past reports along with reports in progress within a fully indexed environment. As a result, an "implicit hypertext" is created that is composed of new reports and the sources upon which it is based (which could include old reports, comments by other managers or links to external Web sites).

Using the MRS is a relatively simple affair. To begin with, users write their reports in MS-Word using a "new report" template. To access the various issues or concerns that may be relevant to the subject of the new report, the user clicks on a "gather issues" button that inserts any such comments into the new report. In addition, the structure service records the links being made between the new report, the transferred issues and the original source reports for these issues that in turn can be "harvested" for future reports. The system also provides a visual tool, in the form of a map, to track the history of a given document through the organization.

The MRS serves as a representative example of hypertext writing within the context of a contemporary business organization and provides a number of insights into the limits of current technology, especially the Web. Furthermore, the system points to the complexity of document creation in today's information-rich environment, implicitly suggesting that hypertext offers a way out of the morass. Such a contention strikes a familiar cord, harking all the way back to the memex, which was also envisioned as a means to confront an increasingly complicated world. While cynics might say that this is merely another case of solving the problems that technology creates with even more technology, it is more informative to position the MRS within the general context of a cultural trajectory that positions technology as a key partner in the continued evolution of the human species. As discussed earlier, this "technoevolutionary" mandate can be seen as central to how hypertext has been conceptualized, developed and applied.

Hypertext at Play

In terms of the relationship between computer games and hypertext, the most direct connection would seem to be around concepts and issues of narrative and the fact that gaming, like hypertext, is founded on forms of interactivity and nonlinearity. Yet, appearances can be deceptive and problematic. Many scholars involved in the emerging field of computer games studies dispute the idea that narrative has anything to do with how computer games actually work and that the academic theories and methods of other disciplines have little to offer game studies and lead to a type of academic colonialism. In his editorial for the inaugural issue of *Game Studies*, Espen Aarseth affirmed that "games are not a kind of cinema, or literature, but colonizing attempts from both these fields have already happened, and no doubt will happen again."[35] Equally suspicious about the motives and relevance of other disciplines is Markku Eskelinen: "It should be self-evident that we can't apply print narratology, hypertext theory, film or theatre and drama studies directly to computer games, but it isn't."[36] Given such comments, I am prone to approach the last portion of this chapter with a certain measure of unease. Although Eskelinen and Aarseth actually temper their initial comments to provide a more inclusive and interdisciplinary approach to game studies, their deliberately provocative statements do raise the important point that games are not like other media and are deserving of their own methodological and theoretical agendas and discourses. Consequently, any discussion about games in a book devoted to hypertext should be approached with a great deal of caution and restraint.

That said, the approach of this final section will be somewhat different from those that preceded it. Instead of offering a selection of examples as a means with which to present and discuss a particular application of hypertext, this section draws its energy from a brief exploration of how the insights and debates within game studies could be used to offer an alternative platform from which to pursue both the study and practice of hypertext in its many forms.

One of the major operative and definitive terms of game studies is that of "ludology." As is usually the case, the term encompasses a broad range of concerns and has also been used for a variety of discursive and ideological purposes, with the aim to establish computer game studies as an independent discipline being among the most central. According to Game Research.com, which is a major portal for the study of computer games, ludology is defined as "the study of game structures (or gameplay) as opposed to the study of games as narratives or games as a visual medium." Far more general is Gonzalo Frasca's definition, who states that "ludology can be defined as a discipline that studies games in general, and video games in particular."[37]

What is notable about the definitions of ludology for the purposes of this chapter is the manner in which they highlight the observation that every medium engenders a unique set of experiential and material circumstances that are intimately connected to content and form. In some ways, this is not only to repeat the standard slogan of the medium is the message, but it is also to affirm the importance of recognizing the materiality of media and the fact that there are concrete and identifiable practices and experiences that arise out of particular media environments. For Katherine Hayles, this necessitates the need for media specific analysis—the recognition "that all texts are instantiated and that the nature of the medium in which they are instantiated matters."[38]

In this chapter's last section, I probe hypertext's relationship to games with a particular eye toward exploring how computer games can contribute to our understanding of the materiality of hypertext as well as the complex relationship among representation, narrative and game play. Among the points I want to stress is that computer games are hardly hypertext's intellectually challenged cousin. Indeed, many important aesthetic and conceptual innovations are occurring within the gaming community that need to be incorporated into the historical and critical understanding of hypertext and digital entertainment in general. In addition, many artists and writers working with hypermedia are as inspired and influenced by computer games as they are by literary, cinematic and artistic traditions and conventions. That said, the study of computer gaming is a distinct area of academic inquiry with its own emerging conventions and methodologies that may or may not be related to the various approaches used by the hypertext community. As has already been noted, there is much debate within the scholarly gaming community about whether or not the concepts and corresponding methodologies of other disciplines such as literature or film have any relevance for the study of games. Such debates certainly distance game studies from normative approaches to hypertext, given the latter's emphasis on narrative and representation as the combined basis for exploring hypertext's potential as a tool for creative expression. Arguably, however, much of this distance is due to the politics of intellectual discourse that tend to favor disciplinary boundaries and formalized institutions. Indeed, as has been argued throughout this book, hypertext is as much an ideological and discursive construction as it is a range of materialized technologies and practice. The contentions over narrative within game studies provide a telling exemplar of such a construction.

Interactive Fiction

The most obvious and persistent starting point for exploring the relationship between computer games and hypertext is via the genre of Interactive Fiction (IF) or Text Adventure. Until recently, interactive fiction and computer games in general have served primarily as a historical footnote in most normative accounts of hypertext and for the most part has been viewed as existing on a lower plane of intellectual, aesthetic and artistic merit. Geoffrey Rockwell, for example, argues that "those like George Landow who have inaugurated the field of hypertext theory tend to treat computer games as lesser forms of hypertexts assuming that what is said about hypertexts applies to computer games."[39] Though often acknowledged as a primitive forerunner to contemporary hyperfiction, interactive fiction or adventure games, such as the eponymous Adventure developed in 1975 by Will Crowther, are generally dismissed out of hand:

> while hypertext fiction has gained some acceptance in academic and literary circles, interactive fiction has usually been dismissed as a triviality. Even worse is the fact that hypertext fiction authors and critics have often quickly joined in its dismissal, sometimes without ever experiencing interactive fiction or after only slight exposure to the form.[40]

Sarah Sloane's assessment of IF is a case in point. In her discussion of the interactive detective fiction *Deadline*, produced by Infocom in 1983, Sloane points out that the main narrative features of IF—"its multiple points of view; its gaps; its multilinearity; its second-person, present-tense address; the limited vocabulary of words recognized from readers—provide a thin and inadequate experience when compared to the reading of print based detective fiction, such as those by Poe, Collins or the experimental prose by Borges and Calvino."[41] Furthermore, according to Sloane, the majority of computer games that are based on the conventions and structures of interactivity are ethically problematic because they "force" readers to partake in acts that they may find "personally repugnant":

> Because the reader resists vigorously the "you" or the self that fiction implies is you, the reader's participation is often reluctant, ambivalent, or culpable. Because she must often commit unconscionable acts to keep the story going, she may assume an attitude of expediency that grates before it comes familiar, when she learns to kill other characters or loot whatever will advance her cause.[42]

Sloane's assumptions here about what the reader finds "repugnant" are not supported by any empirical evidence from actual gamers and seems to reflect rather her own feelings about the acts that she was "forced" to commit while playing games such as *Deadline*.[43] Furthermore, her comments assign literary texts with a de facto moral superiority given that readers are assumed to have a greater degree of freedom in terms of coming up with their own resistant readings of any particular work. Quoting Wolfgang Iser, Sloane argues that readers of interactive fiction (and also hyperfiction) are "unable to read against the code" and "driven to behaviors that many of them would find personally unethical."[44] Curiously, this is an inversion of the central argument often employed to champion electronic textuality, whether IF or literary hypertext. For Sloane, it is the reader's increased agency over the progress of the text that presents a fundamental ethical problem. In my mind, Sloane's argument is limited by her relying too much on literary paradigms to analyze and critique IF and computer games in general. The experience of gaming itself and its particular set of dynamics, conventions and genres are kept in the background. It is certainly possible to "play against the code," but to do so often utilizes a set of techniques and a knowledge base that is distinct from that of print-based culture.

As previously mentioned, Crowther's Adventure is conventionally cited as the forerunner to interactive fiction and computer-based adventure games. Originally written for his two daughters while working as a programmer at the Cambridge-based Bolt, Beranek and Newman (BBN) and based on his experience as a caver, the game was essentially a fantasy version of Crowther's various caving expeditions. The game contained elements of the popular role-playing game Dungeons and

Dragons but for the most part was based on the real world locations of the Bedquilt Cave, which is part of the Flint Mammoth Cave System in central Kentucky. Players of the game were motivated to move through the maze of caves in order to gather up a series of treasure chests. Various obstacles were put in place such as a pirate and poisonous snakes that players had to defeat or avoid in order to move forward. What made Adventure so significant at the time was that players interacted with the computer by typing in simple English phrases or commands, which gave the impression that the player was actually communicating with the computer. One anonymous user cited in Dennis Jerz's Web site recounts his first powerful impression of the game.

> I recall the momentary sense of wonder at this "powerful" program that could understand "GO DOWNSTREAM". And then, I forgot about the programming challenge and was immediately drawn into the story (OK, game). It was my first taste of mimesis. I'm sad for all those who've only experienced the port and not experienced this moment of magic right at the beginning of the experience.[45]

Though the original Adventure did circulate among a few ARPANET sites, it was not until Don Woods, after discovering the game on one of the Stanford Artificial Intelligence Laboratory's computers, modified the program by correcting some of its bugs and adding a greater degree of "magical" narrative elements that basically turned Adventure into a more fully fledged fantasy game.[46]

The graphical interface of Adventure is simple and pared down to the barest of essentials. Interacting with the game consists of typing commands in brief English words; due to the program's inability to "read" more than a few letters, the commands have to be kept very short. Despite such a limitation, Adventure can still offer a compellingly immersive experience by drawing the player into its fictional world. It is this ability to create an immersive and interactive narrative experience that makes IF most comparable and relevant to the community of hypertext scholars and practitioners. However, any such comparisons must be qualified and contextualized. Interactive fictions are *games* and not works of literature, and are thus driven by a very different set of protocols, aims and audience expectations. Furthermore, the nature and function of narrative is also very different (or potentially so) for either media. In an interactive fiction, the narrative is always secondary to the actual game play whereas in a literary hyperfiction, the narrative, however dispersed and fragmented it may be, remains central to the experience. That said, both interactive fiction and hyperfiction are realized within the material substrate of the computer and rely on comparable forms of reader/player agency. In both cases, it is the actions of the reader or player that move the "story" or content forward that in turn immerses the player/reader within the "world" of the experience, whether game based or literary.

The Question of Immersion

It is the ability of computer games to foster high degrees of immersion that I would like to foreground as being of theoretical and pragmatic use to literary (or more generally, expressive) hypertext. My reasons for concentrating on immersion as opposed to a host of other conditions, is that it can be used to probe further one of the central tenets of hypertext discourse, namely that the technology provides an empowering alternative to print media by offering readers the opportunity to engage with a dynamic text that is designed to respond to specific actions, requests and decisions. Among the results is an experience that for die-hard hypertext enthusiasts is considered to be more engaging, more liberating and more immersive than anything the world of print can offer.

The question that I would like to raise at this point is rather simple (arguably simplistic). If immersion (which I am considering here as a generic term that includes also interactivity, engagement and user agency) is a function in both computer games and hypertext (literary or otherwise), which media does a better job? What, for example, provides for a more satisfying immersive, interactive and active experience—a round or two of Grim Fandango, to refer to an old favorite, or an hour spent with Joyce's "Afternoon" or Amerika's *Filmtext*? Be honest.

I am of course comparing apples with oranges and ignoring my earlier assertion that hypertext and computer games serve very different purposes and thus employ tactics and aesthetics that are equally divergent, despite the commonalities that may be found between selected examples. However, my aim here is more in the interest of shifting discursive practices as opposed to defending categories. In other words, I'm moving the pedestals around. As I noted above, computer games have generally been dismissed by the hypertext community as having only an ancillary importance to hypertext development. Added to this is the still lingering sentiment among some critics that whatever can be said about hypertext can also be said about computer games, except that hypertext offers a far more serious and lasting set of examples.

Now imagine the reverse. What if computer games were seen as the standard by which to measure all things hypertext? What if hypertext developers actively pursued the aesthetic and ergodic templates of computer games and applied them to their own work? What would be the result? What could be learned from the experience? To respond to such questions, at least in part, it will be necessary to first qualify what I mean by immersion and how it has been deployed as a discursive and theoretical tool by both the hypertext and computer gaming communities.

For anyone interested in such areas as software design, hypertext theory, virtual reality and computer games, the term immersion should be more than familiar. Yet, as is often the case with such ubiquitous terms, a stable and common definition is often hard to come by. In the case of computer environments, such as computer games and hypertext, immersion is often employed to convey how players or readers can be drawn into the "world" of the virtual environment. Spatial metaphors or concepts figure prominently, such as in the case of Janet Murray who considers immersion to be "the experience of being transported to an elaborately simulated place":

> Immersion is a metaphorical term derived from the physical experience of being submerged in water. We seek the same feeling from a psychologically immersive experience that we do from a plunge in the ocean or swimming pool: the sensation of being surrounded by a completely other reality, as different as water is from air, that takes over all of our attention, our whole perceptual apparatus . . . in a participatory medium, immersion implies learning to swim, to do the things that the new environment makes possible . . . the enjoyment of immersion as a participatory activity.[47]

While certainly evocative, Murray's definition is still a rather sweeping generalization that does not fully account for the complexity of immersive experiences within digital environments. For example, how is it that a graphically primitive game such as Tetris can draw players into its "world" to the point of addiction whereas the rich and evocative world of the Myst sequel Riven leave some players bored and restless?[48] As many have argued, immersion is not just the consequence of realism nor is it solely based on visual and audio environments (recall Adventure). Alison McMahan argues that immersion is the result of three conditions being met within a computer environment:

> 1) the user's expectations of the game or environment must match the environment's conventions fairly closely: 2) the user's actions must have a non-trivial impact on the environment; and 3) the conventions of the world must be consistent, even if they don't match those of "meatspace."[49]

McMahan's three conditions can be summarily described as a form of causality insomuch that users have a better chance of experiencing immersion in environments that "make sense" (once the rules are understood) and that seem to respond in a relatively consistent manner to user input and actions. Once again, there is not one method with which to guarantee such results and, as Emily Brown and Paul Cairns have noted, immersion is not a static concept and is actually not necessary for the enjoyment of a game.[50] That said, in their interviews with game players, they noted that "no one described an experience of immersion that they did not enjoy."

In the case of hypertext, especially literary hypertext, the nature of immersion takes an even more complex and ambiguous turn. On the one hand, hypertext theorists and practitioners have long argued that hypertext offers a particularly engaging experience for readers given its spatial qualities. Michael Joyce's description of hypertexts as being either exploratory or constructive is a well-known definition that in either case describes hypertext environments as spaces that invite active exploration and in some cases augmentation or construction.[51] On the other hand, many literary hypertexts, including those of Michael Joyce, deliberately disrupt the immersive nature of the reading experience by forcing readers to disengage from the narrative by using the program's interface to follow links or to otherwise navigate the space. When compared with computer gaming, this disengagement breaks one of the fundamental rules of effective game play where the "flow" of the gaming experience should be as seamless as possible. Ideally, players should not even notice the interface that they are using to work their way through the game's world. Citing Mihaly Csikszentmihalyi, J. Yellowlees Douglas defines flow as "a condition where self-consciousness disappears, perceptions of time become distorted, and concentration becomes so intense that the game or task at hand completely absorbs us."[52] Although this certainly describes the state of many teenage game players, it is questionable whether readers of hypertext ever achieve such heights of total immersion.

Does this mean that most literary hypertexts are less immersive than computer games and thus not nearly as pleasurable? For Douglas the answer is "yes," but only if aesthetic pleasure is restricted to a conventional understanding of immersion and also if we confuse immersion with *engagement*. With reference to works of classic modernist literature, such as James Joyce's *Ulysses* or T.S. Eliot's *The Wasteland*, Douglas argues that these difficult texts "engage readers deeply because they do not follow schemas for which readers can unthinkingly apply ready-made scripts." Because such texts "violate existing conventions" and thus force readers to rethink existing schemas regarding narrative, plot, characterization, and the like, readers are refused the conventional pleasures of immersion. Instead, however, readers are engaged in a process of discovery and surprise as they encounter new schemas or scripts that Douglas believes to be equally, if not more, pleasurable and meaningful.

> Not surprisingly, engagement tends to be pursued and enjoyed by those who are widely read, since they have access to a vast array of schemas and scripts. Readers who enjoy engagement also tend to enjoy confronting situations for which they lack scripts, as these provide opportunities for learning, as opposed to merely performing one of a series of scripts within a conventional framework . . . The reactions of even well-intentioned critics—witness Murray's "privileging confusion"—to hypertext fiction grows from confusing engagement with immersion, as well as from the fluid, still-evolving nature of schemas and scripts in hypertext narratives.[53]

The not-so-implicit message here is that immersion is rather low brow and that those who seek it via the likes of computer games or a Stephen King novel are not as "well read" or sophisticated as those who seek engagement with works of "serious" hypertext. Intellectual snobbery aside, Douglas's implication here is contentious for two main reasons. First is her insistence that immersion and engagement are two different experiences with the former being clearly inferior to the latter. The distinction between being engaged as opposed to being immersed is not that clear. Brown and Cairns, for example, have identified engagement as being merely the first step toward total immersion that, in fact, lacks the "emotional level of attachment that is seen in later levels of immersion."[54] Accordingly, the characterization of immersion as being a strangely passive state (the result, no doubt of being mesmerized by conventional schemas) when compared with engagement is disputable.

A second concern stems from the manner in which hypertext's inability to engender immersion is the result of the medium's immaturity—"its still evolving nature." Such a sentiment is not without precedent and signals the dominant role of theory as opposed to practice within the hypertext community.[55] Hypertext is essentially being excused for being "too young," thereby deflecting most criticisms with regard to its inability to capture an audience larger than what is currently a relatively tiny circle of enthusiasts. Indeed, hypertext, as will be explored in depth in Chapter 3, is as much a theoretical enterprise (perhaps more so) than a practical one and that any shortcomings can easily be forgiven due to the theoretical sophistication and experimental daring of the individual works. It is, after all, new scripts or schemas that are being pursued here and those that fail to appreciate that should just go back to playing Doom.

I am, of course, being overly harsh here. However, as should be apparent by now, my aim is not to dismiss hypertext but rather to prevent it from being consumed by its own discursive constraints. It is my contention that if literary (or narrative) hypertext is to develop beyond its currently limited state, it needs to seek influences and directives from sources outside of the aesthetics of modernist and postmodernist literature. By virtue of being situated within the digital environs of the computer, hypertext cannot (or should not) distance itself from the rich and complex arenas of digital art and entertainment, which just happens to include the culturally significant area of computer gaming.

Hyperplay: A Few Examples

To bring this section to a close, I discuss a number of hopeful directions—as characterized by a few strategically selected examples—that signal a productive bridge between literary hypertext and computer gaming. In keeping with my focus on immersion, I have selected examples that achieve high levels of engagement with

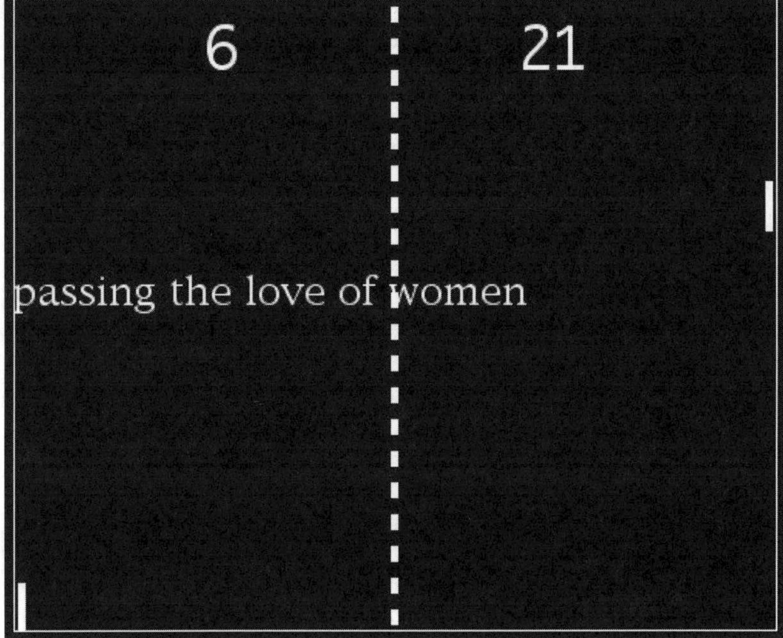

Figure 11. Pong interface in The Intruder by Natalie Bookchin.

their intended audiences and that are not limited to deliberately "difficult" works that require laborious decoding on the part of "well read" readers. Instead, the works that I have selected allow readers or players to effectively interact and engage with the work on the basis of the scripts or schemas that they bring with them rather than forcing them to abandon all familiarity the moment they enter the work. It should be noted that these examples often straddle a number of boundaries and accordingly cannot easily be categorized as either games or hypertext.

A relatively well-known example that can serve as a "template" for probing the explicit use of computer games to structure and deliver a "text" is Natalie Bookchin's The Intruder, created in 1999.[56] The work is based on a story by the Argentine writer Jorge Luis Borges whose work is often cited as a precursor to a host of contemporary phenomena with hypertext and postmodernism being among the chief references. In Bookchin's adaptation, the reader is transformed into a player of classic arcade games such as Pong or Asteroids who "reads" the story by manipulating ten simple interfaces of these early games. For example, the opening scene of the work, shown in Figure 11, features a recreation of the classic Pong interface. In order to read (and hear) the story, the player/reader must successfully play the game, that is, keep the "ball" in motion. Once the sequence is played out, the screen shifts to a new game interface in which the story continues.

The Intruder is difficult to read but "fun" to play. The game interface though simple by today's standards, still requires a level of concentration that distracts the reader/player's attention from the text that unfolds in stutters on the screen and through the speakers. The story itself is presented in a linear fashion and the sequences of the games themselves have been described by Bookchin as presenting "a loose parallel narrative of a history of computer games."[57] In keeping with Bookchin's playful approach, the ability to successfully move through the story may require the reader/player to fail—miss a target, get hit by a falling object, and the like. Thematically, the work explores the relationship between the combat fantasies of most video games and sexual domination, often confronting the player/reader with a disarming mix of irony and critical intervention.

The Intruder employs a number of strategies that connect it to some of the conventions of literary hypertext, the most notable of which is the pace of the narrative being dictated by an interface that demands direct (and in this case constant) action from the reader. Such a demand exemplifies what Espen Aarseth has called the "ergodic" nature of "cybertexts." Briefly, the term ergodic refers to the "nontrivial effort" required on the part of the reader to create a path through a particular text. In other words, the reader must engage in decisions and actions to "traverse the text" in a manner that cannot be accounted for by the definition and concept of reading.[58] Bookchin's work is particularly ergodic because the progress of the text is largely based on the sustained and constant actions of the reader/player. The work also employs the hypertext convention of disrupting the conventions of print literature by constantly frustrating the illusion of transparency, that is, getting "lost" within a narrative's seamless representation of a "world." Despite the fact that the story of The Intruder proceeds in a linear fashion, the relentless interactivity required by the various game interfaces persistently disrupt the continuity of the narrative world. That said, The Intruder, like most games, does provide levels of immersion and transparency that certainly consume the attention of the player, but as Gonzalo Frasca points out, it does so primarily through the powers of simulation as opposed to representation. Unlike narrative media, computer games can be better understood by focusing on their ability to simulate as opposed to representing situations and events. Indeed, Frasca argues that computer games while drawing on narrative representation are based on "an alternative semiotical structure" that "provides a different—not necessarily better—environment for expressing the way we see the world."[59] This "semiotical structure," is different from that of narrative media that is based on "sequences of signs." Computer games and many other "cybertexts" are instead "sign-generators" —they offer models of a particular situation or environment that generate signs according to specific rules created by the designer of the system. In other words, players can always change the "world" of a game by manipulating the game world in a certain way—going west as opposed to east, blowing up monsters, solving riddles, creating new characters and so on. As Frasca notes, simulation is "the form of the future," given that unlike narrative, which deals with what happened or drama which unfolds in present time, simulation deals with "what may happen. Unlike narrative and drama, its essence lies on a basic assumption: change is possible." Returning to Bookchin, what can be said here is that The Intruder while engaging with issues of narrative in a manner that has some connections to similar tactics within literary hypertext, also functions as an exercise in simulation. It is the player's deliberate interactions with the various game worlds and the choices s/he makes that are fundamental to the experience and as such can be better understood through the analytical and critical tools of games and simulation as opposed to narrative and representation.

The experience of hypertext, whether for expressive or pragmatic purposes, is mitigated through the interaction with an interface that, as noted above, is especially ergodic in nature. One must actively engage with the mechanisms of the medium in order to get at its content. It is this central role of the interface that provides another informative and major link between computer games and hypertext. In either case, a reader or player's access to a given text or game is possible only through a particular interface that could be a combination of software and hardware controls and templates. In the case of many of the hypertexts referred to in this book, the primary interface tool is the computer mouse and keyboard and a screen-based system that provides a range of navigation tools, hot links and so on. Computer games employ a similar arsenal of tools that can also include more elaborate controllers such as pistols, joysticks and multifunction devices such as those that come with the Sony Playstation. Generally, the purpose of such interfaces is to allow readers/players to navigate a given hypertext or game and, of course, to dynamically interact with the system. Accordingly, one of the central theoretical concerns within hypertext scholarship has been the discussion of hypertext as a spatial medium that is predicated on materialized navigation and exploration. I deal with this topic in more detail in the next chapter, but for now suffice it to say that space figures prominently in the design and study of hypertext systems and individual works. Furthermore, the "material" nature of the system used to grant access to this space must be considered as integral to the "content" contained within. That said, one of the challenges of creating works that are fully immersive is the design of interfaces and controllers that are essentially transparent and that once understood can be intuitively used by readers or players. Such transparency is evident in The Intruder, given that the general familiarity with Bookchin's game adaptations are grasped almost immediately by the majority of readers/players. Despite the novel and unfamiliar tactic of using the games as a basis for navigating a narrative, The Intruder can still be experienced through the familiar artifice of linear progression, which in this case is driven by the goal-oriented conventions of classic computer games.

Hypertexts that employ the aesthetics and/or structures of computer gaming offer particular insight into the function and role of the interface and the manner in which it contributes to the spatial qualities of the medium. One early and by now classic work of hyperfiction that compels readers to confront the interface is Stuart Moulthrop's "Hegirascope," first published in 1995.[60] The basic premise of the piece can be summed up with the question What if the word will not be still? which is in fact Hegirascope's first screen. Once Hegirascope is initiated, all control over the work's progress is beyond the reader's grasp as there is no interface offered to pause the text as it flashes by on the screen. One immediate sensation is a mild form of anxiety—one had better hurry up and read what is on the screen because it will soon be replaced by another. After the eighth screen, some control is provided to the reader who is faced with a rather standard hypertext configuration of four links. One of these links—"think fast"—serves to remind the reader that this hypertext will wait for no one and that it and not the user is ultimately in control of its progress. While generally characterized as a work of literary hypertext, "Hegirascope" does incorporate the standard gaming device of working to "beat the clock." In this case, failure to keep up with "Hegirascope" will mean that content will be missed. It should be noted, however, that because "Hegirascope" is Web based, readers can always use the standard back, forward and stop buttons of the browser to exercise control over the piece. Such a move, however, could be seen as "cheating" in so much that browser controls are not explicitly part of the "Hegirascope" system or aesthetic. Though a relatively simple work, especially when compared with "The Intruder," "Hegirascope" remains notable as an exemplar of hypertext at play because of its intuitive approach to the spatial and temporal experience of game-like digital environments.[61] The element of time is especially intriguing and as Jesper Juul has noted is central to the gaming experience. In his influential essay "Introduction to Game Time," Juul outlines a distinct model of time in games that in the context of this discussion offers some insight into rethinking the nature of the aesthetics and experience of hypertext.[62] Generally speaking, one of the shortcomings of conventional approaches to literary hypertext is a lack of attention paid to the temporal dynamics of digital environments which allow users to experience a number of temporal conditions. Some of these conditions are the result of the cybernetic nature of the computer, which is to say the possibility for the machine to provide immediate feedback loops. Others are conditioned by the temporal conventions of the genres or forms contained within the computer, such as those of the novel, the film or the computer game. As Juul points out, computer games have been particularly effective in accommodating a range of temporal experiences that often merge seamlessly

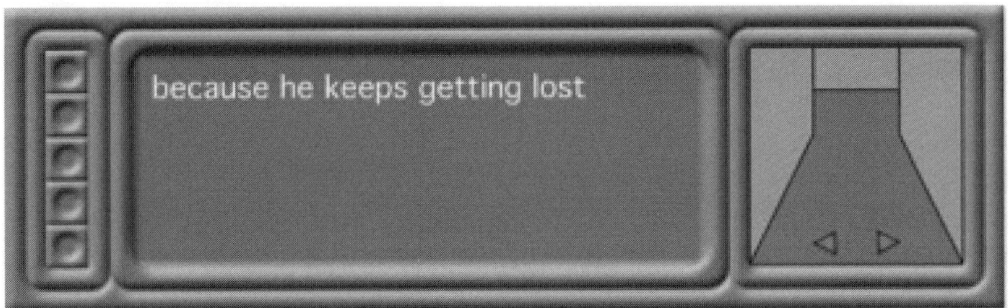

Figure 12. Screenshot of Him.

into one another. Most conventional hypertexts, on the other hand, offer a temporal experience situated mainly with the paradigm of print media. In other words, reading a literary hypertext, such as "Afternoon," is the temporal equivalent to flipping through a dense and complex book or wandering through Borges's "Library of Babel." In contrast, "Hegirascope" provides the extra temporal dimension of machine time that effectively parallels the temporal aesthetics of digital media, especially computer games. It is my contention that this makes for a more engaging and potentially immersive experience than works that are still bound to the temporal rhythms of print media.

A comparable approach is taken by the UK-based artist "Dane" (aka Dane Watkins) whose work "Him" offers a simple console-like interface that allows the reader to view the text and accompanying animations by clicking one of five buttons. The buttons, however, are not labeled nor is there any explanation offered to the reader that may allow for informed choices. In this way, the interaction is similarly dictated by the internal logic of the machine, offering at best an illusion of interactivity and direct agency. The aesthetics of the console and the occasional inclusion of game-like animations, such as the one shown in Figure 12, have the effect of making the experience of "Him" more like a game than a work of "serious" experimental literature. Yet, as with Bookchin, Watkins's playful work is by no means trivial and offers a biting and effective satire of the male psyche and the conventions of masculine success and identity. The text of "Him" is actually a database composed of phrases on male identity cut out from magazines and as such, can be linked to the tradition of "cut up" literature, made famous by William Burroughs. The element of chance is thus of critical import, meaning that some readers might have better luck in encountering readings that are particularly meaningful and rewarding.

Another work that provides an eloquent model for balancing immersion, engagement, interactivity and literary experience is Camille Utterback and

Romy Architu's interactive artwork "Text Rain," which was presented at the SIGGRAPH 2000 convention.[63] The piece is made up of two large screens, which are parallel to one another and thus form a kind of corridor through which visitors must pass. Once inside the corridor, the visitor will immediately notice that his or her image has been captured by a video camera and projected onto the screen in black and white. Also present are colored individual letters, which fall like rain from above and stop once they "land" on the projected image of the gallery visitor. Should the visitor move, the letters continue their descent. What is immediately recognized is that the individual letters can be "caught" via a variety of gestures and objects such as an umbrella, hats or articles of clothing and thus be arranged in ways that may or may not produce snippets of words or sentence fragments. While not immediately apparent, the text of "Text Rain" is not a random collection of letters but actually a poem by Evan Zimroth called "Talk, You" written in 1993. With some luck and agility, fragments of this poem may be captured long enough to be read although it seems unlikely that the complete poem could ever be experienced in its entirety.

As an experience, "Text Rain" is almost immediately satisfying, mainly because of its intuitive interface. No specialized knowledge is required to navigate the work, nor is prior exposure to electronic arts, hypertext or computer games a necessary precondition. One simply walks into the corridor and allows the text to rain down. In his analysis of the piece, Jay David Bolter noted that "Text Rain" was among the most engaging and popular works of the SIGGRAPH conference, mainly due to its providing an accessible and inclusive experience. "TEXT RAIN is not an elite piece of art, but an experience to be appreciated by both construction workers and Ph.D.s in computer science. It manages to be immediately accessible to a broad audience."[64]

Such accessibility, however, should not give the signal that "Text Rain" is merely a form of entertainment and devoid of any conceptual or aesthetic complexity. I would argue that "Text Rain" effectively captures much of what literary hypertext has been trying to do in terms of exploring the dynamics of reading and writing within digital environments, but in a manner that is much more effective and enjoyable. Bolter, in fact, argues that "Text Rain" captures some of the complex and revolutionary aspects of digital art and media, combining "forms or print and video to give us a new kind of reading and writing."

> Digital art, like other digital applications, often opens a window for us, as we look through the computer screen to see the images or information located "on the other side." But TEXT RAIN is also a mirror, reflecting us as we manipulate the letters. It is as if we have passed through the screen and find ourselves inside some malfunctioning word processor that is raining letters down on us. TEXT RAIN surprises and pleases us by being simultaneously

> a mirror and a window. If there is one reason that digital art is important for digital design, it is this: digital art reminds us that every interface is a mirror as well as a window.[65]

The elements of play are also central to the "Text Rain" experience. The work literally invites participants to play with the text—catching it, throwing it, making it into shapes and forms—in a manner that is reminiscent of childhood games such as playing or drawing letters in the sand. I am also reminded of word games and puzzles, such as Scrabble or crossword puzzles that require players to successfully combine letters into words and phrases. Though not exactly a game in any formal sense of the term, "Text Rain" exemplifies what Eric Zimmerman calls "ludic activity or informal play," which is a category that "includes all those nongame behaviors that we also think of as 'playing': dogs chasing each other, two college students tossing a Frisbee back and forth, a circle of children playing ring-around-the-rosy, etc. Ludic activities are quite similar to games, but generally less formalized."[66] It is the ludic nature of "Text Rain" that contributes in an important way to its successful explorations into "new ways of reading and writing," to quote Bolter once again. Equally pertinent is the manner in which "Text Rain" employs what Zimmerman refers to as "dynamic game procedures" to explore the creation and experience of poetic (literary) text in a manner that offers a refreshing alternative to mainstream hypertext fiction and poetry.

For my last set of examples, I turn to Web-based mixed reality games that have provided a complex and diverse platform from which to explore new dimensions in game play, interactive fiction and immersion. These games successfully (and perhaps worryingly) capitalize on the often-fragile boundaries between fact and fiction. In such sites, readers are drawn into the narrative world via a diverse range of Web-based experiences that range from fake Web sites to discussion boards. The "game" essentially becomes the pursuit of the story that develops over time as the various Web sites are updated and augmented by the site creators and in some cases the players themselves. Some of the best-known examples come from the movie and computer games industry that have used such sites to market new products. Steven Spielberg's *Artificial Intelligence*, for instance, was behind the mixed reality game called The Beast, which comprised of over thirty-five individual Web sites as well as mailing lists, voice mail, print ads, TV commercials and live events. The intended result, as Jim Miller notes, was to "create an immersive experience, placing the visitor directly into an Internet-based version of the world envisioned by its creators." Key to The Beast's success was the illusion of the story as taking place in real time, which was made possible by offering the story in a synchronous manner. A similar tactic was used by the creators of the popular game Halo 2, who created the site I Love Bees. As in The Beast, the site offered a range of activities and experiences that included puzzles, telephone calls, fake Web sites and "audio files that, when properly ordered, created a ten-hour audio play related to the story underlying Halo 2."[67] There are two things here that are notable in terms of a hypertext connection. The first concerns the manner in which mixed reality games often serve as vehicles for creating a collaborative community. The second involves how the narrative is often pursued via a complex web of links that utilize a variety of media forms and live experiences. The emphasis on collaboration and community is particularly intriguing in so much that it takes the hypertext tenet of breaking down author/reader distinctions to its limit. While games such as The Beast are certainly created by an identifiable team of writers and programmers, such individuals represent only one side of the total experience. It is the active engagement of dedicated gamers and their creation of ancillary sites (such as www.cloudmakers.com for The Beast), which form an integral part of the total game play and its narrative content. The level of collaboration and the resultant sense of community are far beyond anything achieved under the general umbrella of hypertext-based writing. Much of this has to do with the power of simulation and its uncanny ability to draw participants into an unreal world.

Of course, The Beast is a game and thus driven considerably by the requirement to solve puzzles or riddles. Thus, most of the links or connection points are there for such a purpose. The links in literary hypertext in contrast are not primarily vehicles toward a riddle's solution but rather integral to an associative and evocative structure that is driven by a narrative logic that is often distinct from that of conventional narrative and print culture. While Michael Joyce might object to this, his concept of constructive hypertexts is manifested quite powerfully in the genre of Web-based mixed reality games given their general reliance on both singular and community-driven interaction to perform and structure the overall game environment. In other words, players of such games do actually participate in the construction of the overall experience both explicitly and implicitly. Furthermore, the fact that such mixed reality games often spill out into the "real world," enriches the "constructive" nature even more by way of creating an experience that crosses not only the boundaries between different media, but also the boundaries between mediation and lived reality. For some, this may be a troubling development and lend even more credence to the idea that all computer games are a social evil that will lead the youth of today into a life of antisocial behavior, poor fitness and distorted ideas of reality. But as Barry Atkins points out in his book *More Than a Game*, computer games present no more "a threat to life" than our other fictions.[68] Such arguments, however, are for another book. The point to be made here is that computer games in general offer a vibrant template with which to explore a number of themes and aesthetics that have driven the creation of literary hypertext from the beginning.

Further Reading

Baeker, Ronald. *Readings in Groupware and Computer-Supported Cooperative Work: Assisting Human-Human Collaboration*. San Francisco: Morgan Kaufmann Publishers, 1993.

Bolter, Jay and Richard Grusin. *Remediation: Understanding New Media*. Cambridge, MA: MIT Press, 1999.

Glassner, Andrew. *Interactive Storytelling: Techniques for 21st Century Fiction*. Natick, MA: A K Peters, Ltd., 2004.

Greif, Irene. *Computer-Supported Cooperative Work: A Book of Readings*. San Mateo, CA: Morgan Kaufmann, 1988.

Maeroff, Gene. *A Classroom of One: How Online Learning Is Changing Our Schools and Colleges*. New York: Palgrave Macmillan, 2002.

Meadows, Mark. *Pause and Effect: The Art of Interactive Narrative*. Indianapolis: New Riders, 2003.

Meyer, Katrina. Quality in Distance Education: Focus on On-Line Learning. *ASHE-ERIC Higher Education Report*, vol. 29, no. 4. Hoboken, NJ: John Wiley & Sons, 2002.

Nielsen, Jakob. *Multimedia and Hypertext: The Internet and Beyond*. San Francisco, CA: Morgan Kaufmann, 1995.

Nunberg, Geoffrey. *The Future of the Book*. Berkeley: University of California Press, 1996.

Poole, Steven. *Trigger Happy: Entertainment Revolution*. New York: Arcade Publishing, 2000.

Roberts, Tim. *Computer-Supported Collaborative Learning in Higher Education*. Hershey, PA: Idea Group Publishing, 2005.

Web Sites

ALTX Online Network: http://www.altx.com/home.html

The Association for Computing Machinery Digital Library. Available by subscription only. Public access is often available through university/local libraries. http://portal.acm.org/portal.cfm

Eastgate Systems: http://www.eastgate.com/

Electronic Literature Directory: http://directory.eliterature.org/

Hyperizons: Hypertext Fiction: http://www.duke.edu/~mshumate/hyperfic.html

Poems That Go: http://www.poemsthatgo.com/

Supertart: Hyperfiction Web site: http://directory.eliterature.org/

chapter 3

The Theorization of Hypertext

Hypertext: it's all about the theory. For some readers, this may indeed be the prevailing impression about this thing called hypertext, which ever since the writings of Vannevar Bush has largely been characterized as a potential form rather than something actual and fully developed. Hypertext guru Ted Nelson could be equally dismissed as someone who has spent most of his life in speculation and hyperbole as opposed to in the real world. The hyperfiction crowd is no better, given their tendency to justify their efforts by frequently obtuse and dense references to literary theory and postmodernism. And let's not even mention the numerous software platforms that are now gathering dust in half forgotten drawers. At least Tim Berners-Lee got it right with the World Wide Web. Now, that is hypertext for the real world.

Such statements represent an amalgam of comments and critiques that I have both read and experienced first hand from students and colleagues over the years. While I could dismiss them all by simply stating that they don't really understand what true hypertext is, there is something to the observation that theory has played an unusually large role in the development of hypertext over the years. Indeed, it is this extensive role of theory, especially literary and critical theory that first attracted me to hypertext as a PhD student looking for a dissertation topic. What was so attractive was the idea that hypertext technology offered a "real" platform from which to actualize some of the most central ideas of contemporary literary theory. The title of George Landow's seminal book *Hypertext: The Convergence of Contemporary Critical Theory and Technology*, in fact says it all. Hypertext somehow managed to make theory real and offer "proof" that it actually mattered.

The dominance of theory within the hypertext community may appear to be akin to putting the cart before the horse and in fact detract from an engagement with the actual medium itself, as Marie-Laure Ryan implies in the opening to an essay published in the inaugural issue of *Game Studies*.

> If we compared the field of digital textuality to other areas of study in the humanities, its most striking feature is the precedence of theory over the object of study. Most of us read novels and see movies before we consult literary criticism and cinema studies, but it seems safe to assume that a vast majority of people read George Landow before they read any work of hypertext fiction.[1]

Yet, as I argue in this chapter, the theory of hypertext—and especially the theory associated with literary hypertext—is not merely an appendage or a crutch of some sorts but actually an integral component of hypertext as discourse and as practice. Reading and theorizing hypertext can be understood as being in a symbiotic relationship in so much that for the engaged reader, hypertext theory is part of the total experience. An equally important aspect of hypertext theory via hypertext practice is the idea that hypertext can serve as a kind of "laboratory in which to test" theoretical concepts and moreover to clarify "many of the most significant ideas of critical theory."[2]

> The parallels between computer hypertext and critical theory are of interest at many points, the most important of which, perhaps, is that critical theory promises to theorize hypertext and hypertext promises to embody and thereby test aspects of theory, particularly those concerning textuality, narrative, and the roles or functions of reader and writer.[3]

Landow's idea of hypertext serving as a kind of theoretical laboratory for critical and literary theory is an empowering, curious and contentious statement. It is empowering in the sense of providing critical and literary theorists with, to use Sherry Turkle's notion, "objects to think with" as well as offering a concrete platform from which to present the often difficult and highly abstract concepts associated with the likes of postmodernism and post-structuralism.[4] What is curious, however, is the merger or "convergence" of what would seem initially to be two different spheres, namely literature and computers. At first glance the cold and rational world of computing science and software development would seem entirely at odds with the abstract and decidedly nonpragmatic world of literary and critical theory.[5] For some, however, the merger of technology and theory is highly problematic given that the bulk of the theories used within the context of literary theory were not written with technology in mind and as such could be seen as the type of colonization that Espen Aarseth warns against in the case of computer games studies. The merger also runs the risk of diluting the specificities of various theoretical approaches to a type of general theoretical blanket that can be used to account for almost anything. Thus, the act of taking an idea from Derrida, for example, and "proving" it via hypertext runs the risk of completely disregarding the import of historical and theoretical contexts.

My own take on this matter flits back and forth among the empowered, the curious and the contentious. For myself (and many others, apparently) there is something undeniably empowering or at least satisfying with "seeing" theory actualized in a material and tangible form. At the very least, such "materialization," can provide some concrete form to difficult ideas, which does seem like a good thing. Yet, at the same time, to mix the market-driven worlds of technology and computers with those of the academy seems somehow unnatural and suspiciously like an attempt to legitimate the arts and humanities by aligning it with the seductive allure of high-tech gadgetry and hype. And like Aarseth, I too am troubled by the colonizing ambitions of the academy and the blending of disciplines to the point where everything becomes a postmodern muddle of utterly decontextualized content, form and discourse. Accordingly, this chapter sways between such positions as I present major ideas and statements associated with the fascinating and at times baffling expanse of hypertext theory.

Hypertext: The Unstable, Multiple Text

One of the central concepts associated with contemporary literary theory is the notion that texts—such as a work of fiction, a poem or even a film—are not "stable" entities in the sense of being comprehended by everyone in the same way. Furthermore, to follow a standard line of deconstructionist thought, all texts "undo" themselves by containing within them a host of contradictions and paradoxes that once "discovered" will dissolve the perception of an unified and consistent whole. Such ideas are broadly situated within the critical "genre" (for lack of a better term) known as post-structuralism that has had a profound effect on the practices of literary scholarship and writing. While this is not the place to provide an overview of post-structuralism, what I would like to point out is that it has served as a vehicle for challenging many of the standards and conventions both within and outside of the academy in ways that are often characterized as democratizing and revolutionary. This is relevant to our discussion of hypertext, given similar claims regarding the medium's perceived ability to foster more collaborative and democratic relationships between texts and their readers and writers. Indeed, perhaps part of the lure of post-structuralism for the hypertext community lies in the fact that it can be aligned with parallel aspirations for challenging authority and overturning the "tyranny" of conventional modes of expression and representation.

The French thinker Roland Barthes is an oft-cited hypertext touchstone and in fact Landow makes the claim that Barthes's concept of "ideal textuality ... precisely matches that which in computing has come to be called hypertext." It is worth repeating Landow's quotation of Barthes here at length:

> In this ideal text the networks (reseaux) are many and interact, without any one of them being able to surpass the rest: this text is a galaxy of signifiers, not a structure of signifiers; it has no beginning; it is reversible; we gain access to it by several entrances, none of which can be authoritatively declared to be the main one; the codes it mobilizes extend as far as the eye can reach, they are indeterminable ...; the systems of meaning can take over this absolutely plural text, but their number is never closed, based as it is on the infinity of language.[6]

The above quote does certainly make one think of hypertext, especially given Barthes's use of terms and phrases such as "network," "galaxy of signifiers," and "we gain access to it by several entrances." What else could he be describing but hypertext? Of course, when Barthes wrote this passage, which is taken from his book *S/Z* published in 1970, he did not have technology or computers in mind, much less hypertext. Rather the object of his attention was the literary text, specifically Balzac's story "Sarrasine," in the case of *S/Z*, which was subjected to an evocative and highly complex analysis as a means to reveal the endless possibilities and layers of literature. Critics might well claim that hypertext theorists are taking Barthes's ideas entirely out of context and thus rendering them meaningless. However, such claims are unfounded within the context of literary and critical theory itself, which has served as a powerful vehicle for interpretive and creative acts across a host of disciplines, ranging from film studies to the popular culture. Indeed, it is arguable that the measure of a theory's import or relevance is precisely the ability to use and adapt it outside of its original parameters.

Whatever one's take on this matter, the important point at this junction is the general concept of the fluid, networked, multidimensional text discussed by Barthes and other critics such as Michel Foucault, Jacques Derrida, Gilles Deleuze, Mikhail Bakhtin to name only a few. What unites these various critics and philosophers, at least from the perspective of hypertext, is a shared approach to texts as multiple and dynamic entities that defy single authoritarian readings or interpretations. Landow, for example, notes how Derrida's frequent use of terms such as "link (liasons), web (tiole), network (reseau) and interwoven (s'y tissent) cry out for hypertextuality."[7] Derrida uses such language as part of his project to explore the literary object, particularly the act and experience of writing that serves as a rich vehicle for thinking about the nature of presence—what it means to "be" in the world. What is curious and compelling about the written word (in any medium) is how it allows an individual to enact a "trace" of himself or herself, a literal inscription of a particular expressive act at a particular time. Yet this "trace" is always incomplete, never authoritative because it refers back to something that does not exist here and now. Such is the nature of writing and even more generally language. Words are always defined by other words that in their turn are defined by others. The original, pure source is nowhere to be found. In terms of the literary text, what this essentially means is that any writer, despite his or her efforts to the contrary, can never achieve the possibility of an absolute singularity, which is to say a stable text that means exactly what the writer wants (or believes) it to mean. Thanks to the complex interplay between metaphors, contextual cues and texts of many layers, any work of literature is essentially unstable, thereby engendering a veritable network of meanings and associations.

Multiplicity and Hypertextuality

The application of such concepts to hypertext allows the medium to be characterized as a literal embodiment of multiplicity that is seen as being far more complex and extreme than what exists within conventional linear media such as print, film or television. The main difference lies in what Landow refers to as explicit hypertextuality. Implicit forms of hypertext can be found in nondigital environments, such as any given episode of *The Simpsons*, which are well-known for their references to a myriad of popular culture texts, ranging from Hitchcock's *Rear Window* to the Watergate scandal. It is up to the viewer to recognize the references in order to fully get the joke and so the more familiar one is with past and current media culture, the funnier *The Simpsons* will be. Also, changes in historical contexts will add new layers of meaning to the cultural references within a particular episode that could not have been anticipated by the script writers. However, in a work of hypermedia, the link is explicitly indicated via some type of mechanism such as a highlighted word or image. In this way, readers are directed toward the link, which they may or may not choose to follow. In an imaginary hypermedia version of a *Simpsons* episode, all the cultural references and intertextual moments could be made explicit via some type of interface and even updated to reflect new connections that might exist in the future.

Given the fact that computers can easily handle complex networks of information, hypertext can take the concepts of the multiple, unstable, intertextual text to heights that are simply not possible in print media. "In print fiction," writes J. Yellowlees-Douglas, "a text is all surface. Intention there can be visibly embodied in all the puns, twists, and spins an author can wreak on literary conventions."

> In hypertext fiction, the author both tells a story and designs an experience that unfolds in time—not the fixed and immutable narrative a writer might create in print, but a series of potential interactions that span both time and space. The intentional network—all the structures in the hypertext that either aid or restrict my navigating through it—shapes my

> experience of not only *how* I read but also *what* I read: providing me with paths to follow or words to choose, enabling me to view certain choices and not others.[8]

What Douglas makes abundantly clear—and indeed this is a theme running through the bulk of hypertext theory—is that literary hypertext enhances and actualizes much of what can only be implicitly experienced in print. Thus, the multiplicity that is said to exist within all texts is brought to the forefront by the mechanisms of hypermedia with one result being the creation of an environment that is potentially more democratic and inclusive than linear media. This is partly due to hypertext's greater capacity to incorporate difference and divergence into its formal structure than print.

The "final word" is thus easier to delay in a hypertext given material conditions that favor digression (on the part of both the reader and the writer), divergence and multiple points of view. While technically possible within print media, the physical constraints of the book and the conventions of normative textuality would make such extreme multiplicity quite unwieldy, to say the least. According to Katherine Hayles, digital hypertexts harbor a fragmentation that is "deeper, more pervasive, and more extreme that with the alphanumeric characters of print."[9] Such "depth" is partly the result of the "mutable and transformable" nature of the digital medium itself that one must remember exists as a result of computer code. Hayles makes the valuable point that this code is another crucial level of meaning that most users do not even see. Yet, small changes in that code can radically alter the entire experience of a given digital text. "The layered coding levels thus act like linguistic levers, giving a single keystroke the power to change the entire appearance of a textual image. An intrinsic component of this leveraging power is the ability of digital code to be fragmented and recombined."[10]

Notable here is the manner in which hypertext's mutability is seen as being part of its very essence or nature. It is literally built in, meaning that as a form of media it has a "natural" bias for content that is organized as a network or labyrinth as opposed to a neat corridor that leads from one end to another. It is this bias that has led to claims about hypertext constituting a more "natural" medium for human beings to express themselves with because it more closely approximates how we "really think." The basis for much of this assertion lies within the general condition of associative linking, which is said to approximate or even mirror similar pathways within the human brain. Thus, more linear media, such as print and the conventions around essay writing, are actually restrictive because they go against our innate capacity for nonlinear thinking. Vannevar Bush is frequently cited in this respect, specifically with reference to his famous memex article that is often retold as being a direct challenge to the prevailing technical order by way of suggesting a method of information management that is based on association rather than hierarchies. The memex, according to Bush, would allow users to register their thoughts and connections as they occur in "real time" and thereby become a material parallel to the associative pathways of the user's mind. Much is made of this legacy in contemporary hypertext criticism in the sense that the associative indexing scheme of the memex is characterized as being a radical alternative to the linear models of knowledge, information and organization as represented by the modern state and, more significantly (for hypertext critics), the culture of print. For example, George Landow credits Bush with having produced a "concept of multiple textuality," which amounted to a rejection of some of the "fundamental assumptions of the information technology that had increasingly dominated Western thought since Gutenberg." Landow goes on to say that Bush was motivated by "poetic" aspirations. It was Bush's "wish" to replace the linear methods "that had produced the triumphs of capitalism and industrialism" with what are "essentially poetic machines—machines that work according to analogy and association, machines that capture the anarchic brilliance of human imagination."[11] Such a convergence between the machine and the mind is also celebrated by Dryden who writes: "In its structure of branching links and nodes, hypertext simulates the mind's associative processes, thereby providing an electronic platform for constructing and recording the reader's literate thinking."[12] Such claims though certainly compelling are not without controversy. The theory that the human mind works primarily by association is one that has been frequently challenged within the field of cognitive theory. Equally problematic are claims that the computer can be employed to replicate effectively or at least parallel the human thought process. Within the field of hypertext, Charney has similarly challenged the premise that the associative schemes within educational hypertext are more effective than the assumed linearity of conventional print and points out that hypertext theorists and designers often pursue their work with little or no knowledge of how the reading process actually works.[13]

Hyperconsciousness

Although such debates partially deflate the hypertext balloon, the underlying premise that technology has the potential to alter our consciousness cannot be so easily dismissed. As Landow, via Walter Ong, points out. "Technologies are not mere exterior aids but also interior transformations of consciousness" that impart, albeit in unexpected and often imperceptible ways, fundamental shifts in how societies understand and order their reality.[14] Again, it is important to remember that the discourses constructed around and with technology form as large a part of its "effect" as the material consequences of the technology itself. Consequently, the argument (and belief) that hypertext and digital networks in general parallel how we "really think" might eventually bear fruit because it will lead to the creation of cultural and technological structures that basically affirm it in practice. In other words, if we tell ourselves enough times that something is true, it will eventually be true in the sense of being widely believed and acted upon. What I am describing here is, of course, a very complex and interwoven issue that requires far more room to debate than this book will allow. Suffice it to say that the statements we make about technology and the statements that technology makes for and through us constitute a type of feedback loop that in the end yields the familiar chicken and egg paradox: does hypertext change the way we think? Or has the way we have been thinking given rise to hypertext? Though hardly a satisfying conclusion, my answer is "a bit of both."

Writing the Reader

As already mentioned and partly discussed, hypertext is a medium that radically alters the relationship between readers and writers in a manner that poses serious challenges and alternatives to the very foundations of print culture. "The author of a hypertext," argues David Bolter, "is less a commanding figure than the author of a printed work. For the author's work is not a product of his ego alone; instead, the author works in collaboration with the readers to create the text."[15] Once again, the theoretical impulses of post-structuralism and postmodern theory provide a major theoretical backdrop for assertions regarding the fate of the writer/reader relationship within the hypertext domain. As one might expect, Roland Barthes is a prominent figure here, especially given his famous claim about the "death of the author" and his equally well-known but less provocative distinction between readerly and writerly texts. In the first case, the concept was originally developed in the essay "The Death of the Author," published in 1968 in which Barthes argued that all texts are essentially a network of codes that make concepts such as originality and definitive authorship impossible. "Writing is the destruction of every voice, of every point of origin. Writing is that neutral, composite, oblique space where our subject slips away, the negative where all identity is lost, starting with the very identity of the body writing."[16] At first glance, Barthes's assertion here might appear counterintuitive since he is basically arguing that writing makes the author disappear. Of course he does not mean this literally anymore than the phrase "the birth of the reader must be at the cost of the death of the author" advocates the mass slaying of anyone holding a pen.[17] His point is rather that because all texts are an assemblage of codes that require readers to decode them according to situated and continually developing cultural, interpretive and historical conditions, it is really the reader who has the final "say" in what a text means and not the author. Consequently, despite my own efforts to be clear and to organize my thoughts in a specific way, I, as the author of this book, have absolutely no control over how you, the reader, will understand and use this text. Furthermore, what I experience as my "self," or my conscious presence in time as I think and write this sentence disappears once the sentence is actually written. I am no longer speaking directly to you. Instead, a series of marks on a piece of paper (or dots on a screen) are attempting to speak for me in a manner that, according to Barthes, requires a reader to render back into meaning. To put this as simply as possible, consider the difference between speaking and writing. If I were to speak this sentence to you in person, you would make a direct relationship between my words, my body and my self—you can literally see me speaking my words. Now contrast this to the experience of reading these same words on paper. I am no longer here (or there). My presence is dissolved and there is only you, the reader, who is ultimately responsible for translating these blotches of ink into thought.

The so-called birth of the reader leads to Barthes's important distinction between readerly and writerly texts, which again is frequently cited by scholars of hypertext. Basically the differentiation here is between texts that encourage passive consumption and texts that require the reader to be engaged in an active role of interpretation. In the first instance, readerly texts allow for the experience of *plaisir* that is akin to the simple pleasure of consuming that which is familiar and conventional. Thus, reading a Stephen King novel, for instance is pleasurable because one knows what to expect and thus there is no necessity to disrupt the consumption of the plot with difficult and confusing stylistic or narrative features. Reading something like James Joyce's *Finnigan's Wake*, however, is exactly the opposite experience. Joyce's "novel" breaks so many conventions that readers are literally forced to assume an active role in order to decipher at least a portion of this complex book. Barthes sees the latter as empowering because such works force us to confront our own conventions and do not permit thoughtless consumption. Thus, "difficult" works take on a revolutionary and culturally productive role because they make room for alternative modes of thinking about and representing the world. Again, to bring such abstract thoughts into more familiar territory, think about the last time you saw a film that did not follow many of the "rules" of conventional Hollywood cinema—the films of David Lynch might be a good example. Perhaps you were confused or even angry. But there is a good chance that you may have also experienced a moment of *jouissance*—a type of blissful, energizing "ah-ha" moment—that provided a different and engaging experience of what you know as reality.

The bulk of what we know as modernist literature and art could be characterized as attempts to create such moments of jouissance for its viewers and readers, at least in the sense that many modernist works require the presence of active and engaged readers, viewers and listeners. Literary hypertext, in a way that is probably obvious by now, literalizes the concept of the writerly reader by basically "forcing" him or her to constantly interact with the material on the screen that provides at the very least the illusion of having some control over the final form of the "text." Whether illusory or not, the high levels of engagement required by most hypertexts is generally conceived to be a liberating experience. Ilana Snyder, for example, argues that print literacy was "organized in the service of a dominant author, a god-like figure who was normally male."[18] In hypertext, by contrast, it is the reader who is given a power "that once had been the prerogative of the author."[19] On a practical level, this "power" is often experienced as the ability to read a text in any order, to click on links at random and in some cases to "rewrite" the text by adding new material, links or even reorganizing its structure. It should be noted, however, that for most "classic" literary hypertexts, this last option is usually not made available for readers and that despite the ability to wander around a given hypertext, the work is still the creation of an individual author who has designed the overall system, and thus limiting the range of choices made available to the reader. Indeed, critics of hypertext's overt celebration of the "death of the author" are quick to point this out and argue that the assumed freedom that the reader is said to experience is little more than the ability to make predesigned choices and thus no more democratic than the act of choosing a menu item at a restaurant. The issue here is that choice (or the ability to link) is equated with empowerment and democracy that for Ziegler is a highly problematic concept:

> Central to the liberatory hypertext argument is the "freedom" of the link as opposed to the "closed" form of the book. Whereas Steven Johnson reminds us in his *Interface Culture* that "the link should usually be understood as a synthetic device, a tool that brings multifarious elements together into some kind of orderly unit" (Johnson, 1997: 111), the principle of linking itself for Bolter and Landow seemingly points to the liberty of the individual. However, as we can already see in contemporary consumer culture, selection is usually limited to prefabricated items that contain only a few, easily edible choices (the colors of Nike sneakers, for instance, not the overall design).[20]

Though the "liberatory hypertext argument" warrants suspicion, we should remember that hypertext theory was formed in the heady days before the "dot.com" crash and thus reflects the almost giddy enthusiasm and hope of the period where all things digital appeared to promise something inherently good. Equally pertinent is the impact that literary and critical theory had on the academic community, which as has been noted above, was often employed as a tool for challenging and radicalizing conventional forms and disciplines. In this light, hypertext participates in a wider discourse—one that resonates with the very modern ideals of progress through technology and the continual challenge to the dominance of tradition and convention. That said, the claims around hypertext's ability to reconfigure the way in which we read, write and think are not that easy to dismiss, nor should one strive to do so. Clearly there is something going on that is worth noting and even though the literary hypertexts described in the early works of Landow, Bolter and Joyce did not exactly turn the publishing world upside down, as prophesized by Coover, for example, the arguably "imperfect" hypertext of the World Wide Web has had a major impact. The author is far from dead and the "original work" as defined and defended by copyright laws is also still alive and kicking. But new forms and mutations are all around us—blogs, online games, Web cams and hypertexts to name a few—and they are challenging our legal and conceptual definitions of the text, the work, the author and the reader. Whether this is something to celebrate or not is something that I will leave for the individual reader to decide.

Theorizing Interactivity

The much-vaunted rise of the hypertext reader parallels discussions of interactivity that serves as another major lynchpin in the theoretical canon of the medium. As a term, interactivity is notoriously ill defined and often employed as a catch all to proclaim the benefits of so-called new media. Though definitions abound, Marie-Laure Ryan's four part typology offers what I believe to be one of the more concrete and usable explanations of the concept. Drawing from Espen Aarseth's idea of the cybertext, which will be discussed below, Ryan understands interactivity on the basis of "two binary pairs: internal/external and exploratory/ontological."[21] The first derivation of the pair, "external/exploratory interactivity," characterizes most "classical" hypertext in which "interactivity consists of the freedom to choose routes across a textual space, but this space has nothing to do with the physical space of a narrative setting." Ryan likens such works to jigsaw puzzles in which the text is "a scrambled story which the reader puts back together, one lexia at a time." The reader is thus external to the world of the narrative that cannot be experienced coherently due to its highly fragmented nature. Exploration is thus the only option for interacting with such a text, which is essentially a disorganized database that the reader must "enter" and attempt to comprehend in a piecemeal fashion. The external/exploratory mode "promotes a metafictional stance, at the expense of immersion in the fictional world." Consequently, the bulk of hypertext written in this mode is highly self-referential, fragmented and composed of a "collage of literary theory and narrative fragments." The second form—"internal-exploratory interactivity"—can most commonly be experienced via the genre of mystery or adventure games, with Myst serving as a familiar exemplar. As implied by the term, the user or player can actually inhabit the fictional world but is unable to alter any of the narrative events. Exploration is all that is possible which means that the player or reader is free to move from room to room, pick up objects, interrogate characters or kill the odd monster but all of these actions will not change the content or the world in any substantive form. Ryan's third form—"external-ontological interactivity"—allows the user to assume a god-like role in which he or she has absolute control over the construction of the narrative world and its various elements, features and characters. The most obvious reference here would be the popular game The Sims in which users can define and dictate the behaviors of a large cast of characters as they live out their lives in a simulated environment. For the most part, players though capable of influencing the narrative world are not a part of it and as such, the main character of such a work is really the environment itself or as in the case of The Sims, the totality of all the defined characters and their lifeworld. The final category—"internal/ontological interactivity"—can be described as the holy grail of interactive design and is best represented by an entirely fictional construct: the Holodeck used by the characters of the *Star Trek* franchise. Here, interactivity parallels that of our real word in so much that the "user is cast as a character who determines his own fate by acting within the time and space of a fictional world." The narrative drama, as such, is enacted rather than narrated meaning the player is completely immersed in a fictional world that is in a simultaneous relationship with the player's own time/space continuum. In other words, the player cannot read ahead or look back but only continue with the flow of the world as it unfolds in a dynamic relationship with the decisions made by the player and the system itself. Such an environment remains firmly within the domain of science fiction given the limits of contemporary technology.

What is useful about Ryan's typology of interactivity in terms of hypertext is that it provides a rich palette with which to delineate the nature of the reader/writer/interface dynamic in a way that is not confined solely within debates grounded in (mainly) post-structuralist literary theory. Such a move is productive because it allows hypertext to be explored via a greater range of theoretical models as well as shifts the debate from comparisons between print and hypertext to a discussion that is more inclusive of issues important to the continued development of digital media. The shift away from the comparative mode, in which hypertext always triumphs over print, is especially welcome. There is only so much that can be done with such an argument that while strategic at hypertext's early stage no longer has the same role today, especially given the fact that hypertext has had not nearly the impact on literary production as initially predicted.

The work of the Norwegian scholar Espen Aarseth has also shifted the discussion of hypertext beyond the parameters of literary theory and concerns regarding the altered relationship between readers and writers. Aarseth employs the term "cybertext" that he defines as a "machine for the production of a variety of expression."[22] The term "machine" is not being used as a metaphor "but as a mechanical device for the production and consumption of verbal signs." For Aarseth it is critical for scholars to pay attention to what readers are *reading from* as opposed to only what is being read, as is the case of normative literary theory. Nick Montfort applauds Aarseth for erasing "the stifling hypertext boundary, and to redraw that boundary so that it demarcates a more interesting territory of reader-influenced text."[23] This more "interesting territory" involves the general category of "text machines" that includes but is not limited to hypertext and, moreover, is "independent of the medium in which the work is presented." Thus, a cybertext does not necessarily have to be housed within a computer nor does digital work necessarily fall into the category of cybertext. For Aarseth, one of the defining characteristics of a cybertext is the dynamism that transforms the reader from a mere passenger who "can study and interpret the shifting landscape ... may rest his eyes wherever he pleases, even release the emergency brake and step off, but is not free to move the tracks in a different direction" to "a player and a gambler":

> The cybertext reader ... is not safe, and therefore, it can be argued, she is not a reader. The cybertext puts its would-be reader at risk: the risk of rejection. The effort and energy demanded by the cybertext of its reader raise the stakes of interpretation to those of intervention. Trying to know a cybertext is an investment of personal improvisation that can result in either intimacy or failure. The tensions at work in a cybertext, while not incompatible with those of narrative desire, are also something more: a struggle not merely for interpretive insight but also for narrative control: "I want this text to tell my story: the story that could not exist without me." In some cases this is literally true. In other cases, perhaps most, the sense of individual outcome is illusory, but nevertheless the aspect of coercion and manipulation is real.[24]

Most literary hypertexts are considered by Aarseth to be static in comparison with cybertexts because they consist of links that are preset by the author. Though such links may be of sufficient density and complexity to engender results that the author may not be able to anticipate, they nevertheless are preestablished as opposed to being created on the fly via a cybernetic relationship between the machine and the reader. For Aarseth then, the "machine" (i.e., the computer) becomes an equal player in the author/reader relationship and has a genuinely participatory role as opposed to being a relatively passive object that is primarily a container for content.

Another of Aarseth's useful and well-known terms is that of "ergodic"—a word that is tantalizingly close to the word "erotic," which perhaps contributes to its appeal. Defined as the "non-trivial effort required to allow the reader to traverse the text," ergodic literature requires readers to make explicit decisions about their reading paths. Such decisions may make certain parts of the text unavailable or provide an array of different reading experiences. Most hypertexts are ergodic, often for the simple reason that they require a decidedly nontrivial degree of activity and interaction on the part of readers such as clicking on highlighted words as a means to navigate the work. What is notable about the use of both cybertext and ergodic as critical terms is that they collectively exemplify a "broad textual media category" that is not linked to any one literary genre, aesthetics or set of conventions. Thus, cybertexts, which are ergodic by definition, can run the gamut from the I Ching to online adventure games. As in Ryan's typology of interactivity, Aarseth's terminology is useful because it provides a context within which the dynamics of hypertext can be explored in a manner that "shifts the focus from the traditional threesome of author/sender, text/message, and reader/receiver to the cybernetic intercourse between the various part(icipants) in the textual machine."[25] One immediate result is to downplay the over reliance on literary theory as a prime means with which to conceptualize hypertext, literary or otherwise. For Aarseth this is not intended as an attack on literary theory but rather a move to defend it from becoming "useless" by virtue of being extended far beyond its conceptual borders.

> I wish to challenge the recurrent practice of applying the theories of literary criticism to a new empirical field, seemingly without any reassessment of the terms and concepts involved. This lack of self reflection places the research in direct danger of turning the vocabulary of literary theory into a set of unfocused metaphors, rendered useless by a translation that is not perceived as such by its very translators.[26]

Aarseth is also careful to avoid the celebratory rhetoric of most hypertext scholarship that he equates with a form of technological determinism that makes a direct connection between the technology of hypertext and its assumed ability to engender higher degrees of democracy and expressive freedom. As a result, Aarseth's book is a measured and empirical work that broadens the methodological and theoretical scope beyond those employed by literary analysis and critical theory.

As a means to conclude this section, I should stress that I am not an enemy of literary theory nor do I see its application on hypertext as a grave error of academic judgment. On the contrary, the relationship between hypertext and contemporary literary theory is undeniable and the association between the two areas has spawned a complex range of valuable work, both in terms of scholarship and in the development of hypertext as a genuine literary form. Indeed, as argued at the very beginning of this chapter, hypertext and literary theory are discursive intimates and representative of a shared ideological and historical context that were especially relevant at hypertext's "public" emergence in the mid-1980s.

However, times have changed and hypertext no longer holds the same authoritative status with respect to exemplifying the use of digital technology for literary purposes. Other platforms and phenomena—notably computer games, Web poetry, digital art, the World Wide Web and emerging wireless platforms—offer a far richer and more complex range of ergodic possibilities than what the classic literary hypertexts can provide.

Hypertext and the Networks of Postmodernism

Whether made explicit or merely implied, hypertext and postmodernism have often been grouped under the same theoretical and ideological canopy. While a notoriously slippery term, postmodernism can be understood, for the purposes of this book, as a paradoxical counter force to the aesthetic and historical forces of modernism. It is paradoxical because on the one hand postmodernism seems to contradict much of what defines the modern (and for that matter the whole project of Western enlightenment). On the other hand, postmodernism can be seen as a continuation or even an exaggeration of the modern. The paradox deepens because it is such contradictory directions that are in part what postmodernism is all about. Not being able to define postmodernism is thus very postmodern.

To properly explain and detail the relationship between modernism and postmodernism would require several volumes, and indeed there is a veritable publishing industry devoted to the writing of books and journal articles that attempt to articulate what exactly postmodernism is or could be. To keep things brief and focused on the topic of hypertext, I resort to an admittedly contrived metaphor to outline the major directions and patterns of both the modern and the postmodern and then to draw on the resultant concepts as a way to further articulate the relationship between postmodernism and hypertext and, more importantly, the implications of this relationship. The metaphor employs the artifice of two planets and a shared orbiting moon, which most likely contradicts the laws of physics. On the modern planet we have a society organized around a number of "grand narratives," to use a phrase from Jean François Lyotard who wrote a very influential book on postmodernism in the 1980s.[27] These grand narratives are basically stories that a culture tells itself (through media, history books, political/scientific discourse, etc.) as an attempt to maintain order and to provide a sense of unified historical direction and identity. Two common examples are the belief systems characterized by US style democracy and Communism that both attempt to define and structure a society around an identifiable set of ideas, political ideologies, historical narratives and specific values and standards. The end goal for each case is the creation of a type of universal system that can be used to usher humanity into a higher plane of material and moral existence. Another familiar and potent grand narrative can be found in the twin forces of science and progress that continue to drive how most nations structure the organization and application of knowledge. Under such grand narratives, society and individual human beings can be made stable and ordered. On the macroscale, there is an emphasis or rationalism, functionalism (think of the skyscraper), control, centralization and universal values and laws. In the microscale, individual human beings are viewed as stable unified subjects who are driven by individualism as a means to attain enlightenment, status and self-satisfaction in the world.

The postmodern world, while in close proximity to the modern, is quite different. Here the grand narratives of science, religion and politics have given way to "little narratives," which characterize a far more situational, local, temporary and provisional approach to thinking about and organizing our lifeworld. In this postmodern world, there are no universal structures, theories and ideas that can hope to truly represent or unify everything and everyone. At best, to use the language of so-called chaos theory, all we can do is to identify temporary zones of stability that provide, if only fleetingly, opportunities to make reasonable predictions and to apply provisional standards. This is a world of networks and multinational capitalism where time zones and physical distances are increasingly "overcome" by advanced technology. Individuals within such a world are equally fragmented and are in fact assemblages of various "persons" who "change" according to the needs and requirements of the moment. For example, in one day I can be a parent, a driver, a professor, a husband, a friend, an enemy, a consumer, a citizen, a *Star Trek* fan, a dreamer and a realist. As I pass seamlessly from one role to another, I become, in a sense, someone else meaning that there is no single characterization that can provide an essential definition of who and what I am. One could argue, as Douglas Kellner has done, that contemporary marketing techniques are built precisely on this diversity of roles. For each "self" there is a product, a service or a form of entertainment that best "captures" the essence of that moment and the needs associated with it.[28]

But let's take a look at the shared orbiting moon that is populated by what could be called "aesthetic" formations. When in closer proximity to the modern planet, the moon's formations and denizens favor subjective as opposed to objective experience where individual impressions and states of mind dominate many art forms, especially literature and the visual arts. Realism thus fades away thereby foregrounding abstraction, minimalism or fragmented collages of impressions, feelings and states of mind and perception. There is much blurring of genres and formal boundaries. High culture and low (popular) culture merge into one another; novels, for example, no longer follow the structures and conventions of the nineteenth century. The new is generally celebrated or at least brought into the spotlight and many are inspired by the achievements of modern engineering and science. Among the citizens who populate the modern moon are Pablo Picasso, James Joyce, Gertrude Stein, Virginia Woolf and Le Corbusier.

When the moon gravitates toward the postmodern world, things appear on the surface to be quite similar. Here we can also find fragmentation, the merger of the high and the low, the lack of genre distinctions, discontinuity, ambiguity and bricolage. There is a greater emphasis on irony and pastiche and the denizens of the postmodern moon seem to be generally more irreverent and playful than their modern manifestations. Moreover, they seem to be far more accepting if not celebratory of the fragmentation that defines their environment. If one recalls some of the work of the great modern novelists and poets (such as Eliot's *The Wasteland* or Camus's *The Stranger*), it becomes apparent that the loss of the central, unified self and the rapid changes of the modern condition are something to be mourned and represented as a loss. Whether as represented through Chaplins's *Modern Times* or the stories of Jorge Luis Borges, modern life is ultimately alienating and destructive. It strips us of our human essence.

On the postmodern moon, however, there appears to be a continuous party. The fragmented nature of contemporary life if not overly celebrated is at least accepted and used as a means to express oneself. While there is certainly a sense of loss and critique, the postmodern condition generally adopts more cynical, nostalgic and ironic tones, with humor and parody being stylistically dominant. Think of David Lynch, Salman Rushdie, Douglas Coupland, Cindy Sherman, Jeanette Winterson to name a few. These filmmakers, writers and artists do not shy away from critique nor are their works all positive and cheerful representations of postmodern life. Many of the stylistic and formal techniques of their modernist compatriots are utilized but throughout much of their work and the work of other postmodern artists, thinkers and writers, is a vein of playful irony and critical distance that provides a flavor that is distinctly different from the central works of the modernist period.

Hypertext has a resolute and definite home on the postmodern moon despite taking a number of cues from modernist predecessors especially in the case of literary hypertext. As a form of representation and expression, its dynamic of fragmentation, linking, association and boundary breakdowns would seem to make it the ideal "engine" for postmodern reading, writing and thinking. In addition, hypertext makes explicit the connection between technological media and what Rob Witting called "habits of mind" which is to say the assemblage of conventions, codes and practices that constitute normative patterns of individual and social discourse, articulation and representation.[29]

To think through such a claim, a few ideas from Fredric Jameson's important and by now canonical work *Postmodernism: Or the Cultural Logic of Late Capitalism* are informative. One of Jameson's essential claims is the argument that modernism and postmodernism are linked to the cultural formations of modernity and postmodernity.[30] The basis difference between these two sets of terms is that the modernism/postmodernism distinction describes largely aesthetic and cultural formations whereas the dualism of modernity/postmodernity is indicative of much longer historical trends and developments that are the result of identifiable ideologies, politics, historical circumstances and technologies. Jameson outlines three stages that represent the evolution of the modern into the postmodern.

1. Market capitalism: Eighteenth and nineteenth centuries.
2. Monopoly capitalism: Late nineteenth and mid-twentieth centuries.
3. Multinational or consumer capitalism: Late twentieth century to the present.

What is notable about Jameson's stages for our purposes is the emphasis on technology as being among the primary forces that shape each of the three stages. For the postmodern age, the computer is a dominant force and is often seen as a key representative in terms of its basic characteristics and features, especially around concepts of the so-called Information Age.[31] Accordingly, it is not hard to see how hypertext can be thought of as a definitively postmodern form, especially around the characteristic of playful fragmentation:

> Seen from the viewpoint of textual theory, hypertext systems appear as the practical implementation of a conceptual movement that coincides with the late phase of modernity. This movement rejects authoritarian, "logo centric" hierarchies of language, whose modes of operation are linear and deductive, and seeks instead systems of discourse that admit a plurality of meanings, where the operative modes are hypothesis and interpretive play and hierarchies are contingent and local.[32]

Moulthrop's conflation of hypertext with "the late phase of modernity" (i.e., postmodernity) is an obvious reference of Jameson. As a technological system, hypertext not only represents but also embodies postmodern characteristics and, as such, can be employed to elicit discussions and critiques of a decentered, fragmented state of being where conventions regarding the experience and nature of reading, writing, subjectivity (identity), representation and truth are radically challenged and altered (frequently for the better). Frequently this radical challenge is actualized around what I call the "spatial turn" of postmodern thought, which takes on a very particular and informative characteristic in the case of hypertext and, more generally, digital information technology.

Within postmodern society, as David Harvey, among others, has asserted, space and time have become compressed to the point where our experiences of either are radically different from those of previous generations.[33] A similar point was made even earlier by Harold Innis, whose differentiation between time-bound and space-bound societies clearly articulates how contemporary society is increasingly structured around technologies that "spatialize" or abstract material reality to the point where embodiment is no longer a necessary condition for presence and agency. Such spatialization or compression of temporal and spatial experience can be related to the postmodern characteristic of overt commodification through which everything, whether material or immaterial, is deliberately marked for potential inclusion into the marketplace. The conditions of postmodern capitalism, or "disorganized capitalism," favor exactly the kind of paradigm made explicit by hypertext. Johnson-Eilola writes,

> We can see vividly ... the ways in which technologies develop and are used along lines of existing cultural force; although many hypertext theorists from the composition and literature disciplines assert a hypertext that displays openness, multiplicity, blurring roles, and other postmodern tendencies, that very fragmentation and sliding control are shaped by the forces of (disorganized) capitalist production and marketing. The historical commodification of information in other media provides a clear precedent.[34]

One of the things made clear by Johnson-Eilola is that hypertext can be aligned along the historical continuum that, as Jameson has argued, situates specific technologies within the cultural and economic logic of a particular age. Thus, to put it very simply, hypertext coincides with the impulses of postmodern capitalism and the information economy that currently dominates present day culture and society, and represents, as Jay Bolter has claimed, an important stage in the continued evolution of the mind/machine relationship as actualized within specific historical spaces and their concomitant mediation.

Hypertext and the Network Age

The alignment of hypertext with historical and ideological contexts necessitates that the celebratory rhetoric of hypertext and its association with democratic principles be tempered with the realization that this same technology is also part of what Castells identified as a new historical condition in which "productivity is generated through and competition is played out in a global network of interaction."[35] Of course, it is important to emphasize that global capitalism and our so-called information society or network age are not evil, oppressive entities by definition nor that my connection between hypertext and the forces of contemporary economics implies some kind of moral lapse on the part of the hypertext community. At the same time, however, to view hypertext technology as a medium for emancipation is dangerously naive, mainly because it ignores the specific social, economic and political contexts that allowed it to be developed in the first place. We can recall the earlier discussion of Andrew Feenberg's "technical codes," and his understanding of technology as a "scene of structure," and a "parliament of things on which civilization alternatives are debated and decided."[36] Neither neutral nor inevitable, technology is thus better understood as a constellation of paradigms, values and techniques that both informs and is informed by what might be crudely referred to as "real-life" cultural/social practices and models. It follows that enquires into the so-called effects of technology on society should not be concerned with one-dimensional relations of cause and effect but rather with a multidimensional model of social and cultural agency where technology is but one member of an increasingly diverse cast of actors.

As one of these actors, hypertext corresponds to what I have elsewhere termed the "digital paradigm" that can be briefly summarized by the following "digital codes" for individual, social and cultural relations and practices[37]:

1. Extension/augmentation: While applicable to technology in general, the type of extension or augmentation possible via the digital is both physical and mental. It can be used to transcend both the limits of the body and the mind. To be digital is thus often described as being more than human—for example, the posthuman or cyborg.
2. Fragmentation: Nonlinearity as the dominant format of digital spaces, epitomized for the moment by the hypertextual domains of the World Wide Web. The resultant fragmentation has implications for expression, representation and, ultimately, cognition.
3. Mutation: The seamless "morphing" of one state, one condition into another eradicates any notions of authenticity and perhaps even progress or evolution. As such, the only constant is change, which has countless directions.
4. Hypercontextualization: The possibility of endless and "inconsequential" changes, mutations, revisions and fragments subordinates content almost entirely to context. Meaning is thus removed from the message and contained, rather, within the ever-changing interaction between context and message.
5. Anti-body: With the body and mind extended or augmented, the mind tends to win in the end. The body is not suited to the demands and pleasures of the digital, the cyber. It is mere "meat," a primitive holdover from the predigital past.

These digital codes, as I call them, resonate with the discourse of postmodernism as well as indicate the manner in which "our societies are increasingly structured around a bipolar opposition between the net and the Self."[38] Such an opposition is indicative of what could be understood as the foundational function of the Net with respect to its role in informing the nature of individual and social being. Hypertext is again representative of how it articulates this so-called opposition and in how it employs it as a means to theorize the conceptual and material modes of individuality and subjectivity (as represented most significantly by the writer/author dualism). In this way I replicate the discourses that articulate the transformative nature of digital/information technology with respect to fundamental notions and practices of identity and community. Representative here is Mark Poster's thesis that electronically mediated communications enact "a radical reconfiguration of language, one which constitutes subjects outside the pattern of the rational, autonomous individual."[39] For Poster, the "mode of information" as represented by hypertext technology, signals a radical break with modernist (i.e., humanist) models of subjectivity and the social order constructed around it. In the case of hypertext, this "break" is frequently celebrated and employed as a means to create empowered forums for exploring alternative forms of identity and discursive constructions. One telling example is Wendy Morgan's paper entitled "Electronic Tools for Dismantling the Master's House: Poststructuralist Feminist Research and Hypertext Poetics." The title alone reveals the familiar convergences among hypertext, literary theory and postmodernism. It also speaks to the belief in hypertext's radicalizing potential, which harks back to the early musings of Ted Nelson. In short, hypertext can change the world, or to follow Morgan's more modest assertions, at least productively destabilize the certainties of the status quo:

> [Hypertext] offers post-feminist writers a species of "deterritorialised" writing. It may be used as a more collegial space, in which voices can speak to and with one another across what had been static boundaries. It may be used to create an intricate network of a text whose intertextual complications demonstrate how impossible it is for a single account to claim definitive authority. It may become a space in which text is juxtaposed with dissenting text to create sparks out of their friction. And even where there are such disagreements, a hypertext may choose not to privilege one account over another by placing the less favored version as a subordinate paratext. In such ways post-feminists may choose to deconstruct the singularity of their own position. And so they may perform their understanding of how we are each multiple selves: subjects woven out of diverse discourses.[40]

Morgan's reference to Gilles Deleuze's concept of deterritorialization indicates the "spatial turn" referred to earlier in which hypertext is being positioned as a "writing space" where boundaries are continually dissolving as (digital) signifiers spin and weave themselves between writers and readers. Yet, while such "deterritorialisations" may well serve the needs of postfeminism and other intellectuals interested in challenging stagnant discourses, it must be remembered that postmodern capitalism is equally driven by the collapse of boundaries, whether discursive, spatial or material. Thus, in addition to empowering free thinking academics, hypertext can just as well play into the needs of what Arthur Kroker has cynically dubbed the "virtual class." In this case, capitalism, consumerism, identity and technology are tightly wired together, thereby promoting a world view and concomitant ethical system that is forever contained within the technoeconomic loop.

> Far from having abandoned ethical concerns, the virtual class has patched a coherent, dynamic, and comprehensive system of ethics onto the hard-line processors of the will to virtuality ... Against democratic discourse, the virtual class institutes anew the authoritarian mind, projecting its class interests onto cyberspace from which vantage-point it crushes any and all dissent against the prevailing orthodoxies of technotopia.[41]

Such a technotopia and its corresponding "econotopia" results in, according to Kroker, a "reduced vision of human experience." In this respect, the human subject is mutated, reconstituted, refigured or otherwise altered in such a way that any locus of definition and relevance is increasingly tied to the continually shifting context of the digital marketplace. For many, this is a cause for celebration, for visionary exclamations of a bright and profitable future. Take for instance, *Wired* magazine's editor Kevin Kelly who, in a 1997 feature article, boldly outlined the "new rules for the new economy." Amidst such numbing aphorisms as "embrace dumb power, make virtuous circles, follow the free and feed the web first," Kelly repeatedly states that digital technology, in its various forms, is fundamentally altering human experience and meaning. In one passage, the Net is characterized as "the collective interaction spun off by a trillion objects and living beings, linked together through air and glass." In another, the assertion is put forward that the "frontier feel" of the Web is due to the fact that this is "the first time in history [that] we are witnessing biological growth in technological systems." Such thoughts lead eventually to the somewhat eerie conclusion that the "wonderful news about the Network Economy is that it plays right into human strengths. Repetition, sequels, copies, and automation all tend toward the free, while the innovative, original, and imaginative all soar in value." More than implied here is the assumption that the standards by which all things should be measured against are resolutely economic in nature and, moreover, within Western models of technological development, value and subjectivity. Thus, for Kelly and the rest of the *Wired* generation, the order of the day is to mutate, to become one with the Net, to forsake the analog world of atoms and to become the new corporate citizens of the digital world.

Many of the hypertexts that I have referred to in this volume, particularly those with literary and artistic ambitions, would appear to be worlds away from the corporate agendas elegized by Kelly and other like-minded boosters of the so-called new economy. Yet, as I have tried to make clear, hypertext like any other technological formation, is deeply situated within a historical and ideological context that has and continues to inform its many incarnations. While the use of literary theory, post-structuralism and postmodernism provide templates with which to explore and emphasize the emancipatory potential of the medium, it must be remembered that these same theoretical discourses—with postmodernism leading the pack—also inform the "habits of mind" associated with contemporary mainstream culture and the economic and political engines that drive it. This leads to the familiar scenario of the double-edged sword, which in this case involves one side being used to cut a swathe through the conventions of the status quo and the other being to cut an even larger swathe in order to plant the seeds for a new status quo altogether. One inevitable question is which side is "better"? Another less obvious question asks whether there is really a difference between the two sides once everything has been cut down? I have no answer at this point, although the following passage from Michael Joyce echoes one of my more likely responses.

> I console myself with knowing that no one around me seems to have any more satisfactory answers: neither the media giants who would make presumptive claims on network culture if they could decipher its nature and whose business it is to do so, nor the networked culture of artists, critics, theorists whose glimpses feed me and whose gestures I follow like a man dancing with shadows. I still throw in my lot with the latter, of course, because as my prefatory meditation here notes, I love shadows and trust outsiders.[42]

Further Reading

DeRoure, David and Helen Ashman. Eds. *Hypertext 2004 Proceedings*. San Antonio, TX: Association for Computing Machinery, 2004.

Landow, George. Ed. *Hyper/Text/Theory*. Baltimore: Johns Hopkins University Press, 1994.

Landow, George. *Hypertext 3.0: Critical Theory and New Media in an Era of Globalization*. Baltimore: Johns Hopkins University Press, 2005.

Lanham, Richard. *The Electronic World: Democracy, Technology and the Arts*. Chicago: University of Chicago Press, 1993.

Leeson, Lynn Hershman. *Clicking In: Hot Links to a Digital Culture*. Seattle: Bay Press, 1996.

Manovich, Lev. *The Language of New Media*. Cambridge, MA: MIT Press, 2002.

Moulthrop, Stuart. "You Say You Want a Revolution: Hypertext and the Laws of Media." *Postmodern Culture*, vol. 1, no. 3 (May 1991) http://www3.iath.virginia.edu/pmc/text-only/issue.591/moulthro.591

Sloane, Sarah. *Digital Fictions: Storytelling in a Material World*. Stamford, CT: Ablex Publishing, 2000.

Taylor, Todd and Irene Ward. *Literacy Theory in the Age of the Internet*. New York: Columbia University Press, 1998.

Ulmer, Gregory. "Grammatology Hypermedia." *Postmodern Culture*, vol. 1, no. 2 (January 1991).

Web Sites

Bernstein, Mark. "Patterns of Hypertext." http://www.eastgate.com/patterns/Patterns.html

Cyberspace, Hypertext and Critical Theory. Maintained by George Landow.http://www.cyberartsweb.org/cpace/

The Electronic Labyrinth. http://www3.iath.virginia.edu/elab/

chapter **4**

The Future of Hypertext

What does the future hold for hypertext? The response, of course, depends on how you would define hypertext and also on what you would consider as appropriate uses of the technology. If HTML embodies the essence of hypertext, then the future looks very bright in the sense that the World Wide Web is showing no signs of disappearing anytime soon. However, if you have every title published by Eastgate Systems on your shelf (and in your computer) you may have the sinking feeling that the days of "serious hypertext" are seriously numbered. The situation for educational uses of the technology presents somewhat of a mixed bag. On the one hand, distance learning is still touted by university administrators as a viable (and profitable) road to higher learning and the World Wide Web holds a prominent place within most contemporary educational institutions, from the kindergarten to the graduate seminar. On the other hand, the types of "electronic classrooms" that allowed for multilevel, cooperative and nonlinear writing environments have not exactly replaced brick-and-mortar institutions. So all in all, hypertext, at least as envisioned by Ted Nelson and celebrated by hypertext theorists such as Landow, Joyce and Bolter, appears somewhat tattered and dated. The excitement has certainly faded into a malaise that the engines of big business and the entertainment industry have clouded hypertext's brief moment in the sun.

So once again: does hypertext have a future? As you may suspect, the answer is both yes and no. It is clear that the types of nonlinear, user-driven environments characterized by the World Wide Web and most computer games offer compelling evidence that hypertext is one of the primary engines of contemporary forms of representation, expression and information management. Yet, the revolutionary claims of early hypertext theorists and the notion that hypertext will replace print (or linear narrative media) has clearly not come to pass. Especially shaky is hypertext's position as an emancipatory vehicle for literary expression that no longer has the same theoretical cache that it had in the early 1990s. As Robert Coover laments, the golden age of hypertext is over.[1]

In this final chapter I probe the apparent decline of hypertext, especially in terms of its uses as a vehicle for creative (literary) expression and as a platform for theorizing the nature of reading/writing and the concomitant roles of the reader/writer. What should be made clear, however, is that my aim is not to engage in a form of critical finger pointing where literary hypertext and the theories associated with it are sent to the landfill of outdated ideas. Such a move would not be productive by any means. Rather my aim is, as stated in the introduction, to emphasize hypertext's important theoretical legacy for the continued exploration of digital media. What is still highly relevant about hypertext scholarship and creative practice is the manner in which it offers a highly developed and consistent approach to thinking about how a medium alters some very fundamental aspects of human expression, representation and comprehension. Hypertext also marks one of the first forays by humanities-based scholarship into an active (i.e., not just theoretical) engagement with digital media technology and thus serves as an important precedent and model for like-minded forays in the future. As such, there is still much to be learned from hypertext, both in terms of its apparent failings and its innovations.

That said, my final thoughts on the future of hypertext will take an initial cue from Robert Coover's lament regarding the passing of hypertext's golden age. Near the end of his keynote address, Coover notes that the "noisy, restless, opportunistic, superficial, e-commerce driven, chaotic realm" of the World Wide Web has essentially driven the literature away:

> Literature is meditative and the Net is riven by ceaseless hype and chatter. Literature has a shape, and the Net is shapeless. The discrete object is gone, there's only this vast disorderly sprawl, about as appealing as a scatter of old magazines on a table in the dentist's lounge. Literature is traditionally slow and low-tech and thoughtful, the Net is fast and high-tech and actional. As for hyperfiction, the old golden age webworks of text have largely vanished, hypertext now used more to access hypermedia as enhancements for more or less linear narratives, when it's not launching the reader out into the mazy outer-space of the World Wide Web, never to be seen again.[2]

Yet all is not lost. "Poetry," claims Coover, "has indeed prospered in this new medium, even more than fiction." Among the reasons is the premise that the interlinked, multidirectional, mobile and fluid nature of the Web provides a more "congenial" atmosphere for poetic expression, because it is not as tied to the conventions of linear narrative.

> With hypermedia, a whole new poetic movement has emerged, called kinetic poetry, or poetry that "moves," in which the text of a poem undergoes ceaseless transformations on the screen, emerging and disappearing, evolving into shapes and motions and patterns

> that "imitate" the poem itself, interacting visually with other elements of the poem or aurally with overlaid sound files. Visual artists sometimes even insist on calling their own hypermedia works "poems," though they may contain few words or none at all, keeping poetic structures intact but displacing language with visual images.[3]

Coover's observation regarding the healthy state of poetry, however broadly defined, within the hypermediated context of the Web, provides further credence to my argument that many of the practical and theoretical acts pursued under the domain of hypertext may be greatly enhanced by looking to the wider terrain of digital media, art and entertainment. Equally productive, as demonstrated by the more recent work by Espen Aarseth, Jay Bolter and others, is the integration of conventional hypertext "concerns" and theoretical discourses with those that look beyond the concerns of reader/writer relationships or the manner in which media technology affects the nature of narrative. One of the "problems" with hypertext, at least in terms of it maintaining its relevance, is that there has been an overriding emphasis on situating the medium primarily within the local of literary narrative or fiction. Though a number of scholars certainly consider the specificity of the medium in a manner that parallels the "material turn" discussed above, paradigms of literary narrative remain at the core. So while Bolter may indeed argue that hypertext is topographic and more reliant on spatial and visual paradigms, the discussion for the most remains situated against print. The book is always considered hypertext's opposite and celebrated because of this opposition. Likewise, the oral tradition is favorably compared with hypertext, which engages in the familiar dichotomy (as identified by Derrida and lamented long ago by Plato) between the voice and text, with text being on the side of the "bad" or the "dead." Among the effects of such tactics is to forever revisit issues concerning reader/writer dynamics and the nature of narrative in the digital era. Equally problematic is the continued reliance on literary theory (especially post-structuralism) as the primary base for theoretical work on the medium. While the use of literary theory has indeed led to some important work and insight, I maintain that the time has come to move the discussion into a wider discursive terrain that looks beyond narrative as the best way with which to explore the nature of expression and representation in the digital era. Hypertext still matters, but only if it is informed and developed by being situated outside of the boundaries that have conventionally defined it as a topic of academic inquiry.

The work of Marie-Laure Ryan provides a valuable resource for continued work in hypertext scholarship, at least if confined to the humanities. Also important is the collaborative work of Jay Bolter and David Grusin, Katherine Hayles's recent work on media specific analysis and the theoretical directions of scholars such as Mark Hansen who emphasizes the need to consider the material and phenomenological nature of technology and its participatory role in defining what we experience as "reality." What is exemplary about these scholars is a shared desire to probe our experience with technology (mainly media technology) from perspectives that for lack of a better term could be defined as "physical" or "material." Such an interest in the physical and material prompts us to understand media technology as having an active role in the construction of what we, as human beings, experience and comprehend as reality. Hansen, in particular, argues that technology is essentially a "material force of natural history" because of its role as an "agent of material complexification" that requires a "corporeal and physiological adaptation" on the part of both human beings and the general environment.[4] Such an approach redirects methods of critical and historical inquiry beyond the discursive and rather toward what Hansen describes as a physiological approach. Such an approach brings, according to Hansen, much needed emphasis on the degree to which "technology impacts our experience first and foremost through its infrastructural role" and the manner in which it "informs our basic ways of seeing the world."[5] Technology and humanity thus become part of the same dynamic bundle, making it difficult if not impossible to separate one from the other or to understand one as preceding the other.[6] What this means in the context of the present topic is that hypertext takes on the function of a material presence that potentially alters the trajectories of both human society and technological development. Although this may seem overly complicated, the point here is actually quite straightforward. Hypertext, like any technology, is part of the real world both in terms of having a material presence and in terms of being part of the general matrix of human activity and culture. Thus, the act of thinking about and theorizing hypertext requires one to consider not only the specific material conditions of the medium and its relationship to prior modes, such as print, but also to realize that hypertext is situated within a very complex dynamic that is beyond the ability of any one disciplinary area to fully capture. A sentence from Katherine Hayles's brief but highly informative and evocative book *Writing Machines* is worth repeating at this juncture: "Medium and work were entwined in a complex relation that functioned as a multilayered metaphor for the relation of the world's materiality to the space of simulation."[7] Hayles wrote this passage in response to her reading of M.D. Coverly's hypertext novel *Califia* that prompted a type of theoretical epiphany through which she realized that her reading of *Califia* was initially limited by the fact that she was focusing on the words alone rather than "from an integrated perspective in which all components became signifying practices." These components included not only the text, of course, but also the "layered images, complex navigation functionalities, and simulated documents."[8] Such thoughts led to Hayles's concept of media specific analysis that argues for the need to consider the material conditions of the medium as well as the content when engaging in any form of analysis or critical reflection. Based on the preceding discussion of Hansen, I advocate that Hayles's approach be augmented by considering also the material conditions and dynamics between the medium and the "world" in which it is situated. Thus, considering the material specificity of hypertext involves also the consideration of topics such as the information economy, the technological infrastructures of a given society, the dynamics of human-computer interaction, the environmental consequences of information technology and the ideological conditions around which particular technologies were brought into being and others were left to fade into obscurity. This list could extend into infinity which might lead one to argue that what I am proposing here is a practical impossibility. However, my point is not to encourage forms of scholarship that attempt to be utterly comprehensive in terms of taking everything into consideration. Such a task is reminiscent of one of the unfortunate characters in a Borges story who toils away at projects that literally have no end. Rather, my aim is to draw attention to the rather simple concept that the material conditions of a particular medium extend far beyond the specific confines of the technology and also involve the materialities of the world itself.

Thus far, my remarks concern primarily the future of hypertext scholarship in so much that I have been concerned with probing analytical and theoretical models that I deem to be more appropriate in the present circumstances. Yet, my remarks about the need for considering wider spheres of material conditions can also be used to extend our concepts of what hypertext has become or is on the way to becoming. Hayles uses the term "second-generation electronic literature" to describe works that extend the possibilities first explored in works such as Joyce's "Afternoon" or Moulthrop's *Victory Garden* that in general emphasize the link as the primary mode of engagement on the part of the reader. Second-generation electronic literature, as represented by works such as Mark Amerika's *Filmtext* or Talan Memmott's *Lexia to Perplexia*, generally incorporate a greater palette of resources that include but are not limited to sound, images, code and radical interfaces. Hayles coins yet another neologism to describe this new generation:

> Technotexts: when a literary work interrogates the inscription technology that produces it, it mobilizes reflexive loops between its imaginative world and the material apparatus embodying that creation as a physical presence.[9]

Hayles's term takes its cues from the neologisms of other like-minded scholars, notably Espen Aarseth's "cybertext" and Bolter and Grusin's "remediation" who each in their own way emphasize the need to confront material conditions and the complex interplay among content, technology and form. Terminology aside, the essential point here is that the practice of hypertext is indeed alive and well; however, it is increasingly mutating into forms that are a far cry from the type of work described by early hypertext theorists. Comparing Memmott's *Lexia to Perplexia*, which Hayles carefully analyses, to "Afternoon" reveals a startling change of trajectory. Joyce's work can be clearly situated in the sphere of experimental literature and thus understood and appreciated primarily via its relationship to and departure from narrative conventions.[10] *Lexia to Perplexia*, however, is something quite different. With its shifting, restless interface and automated sequences, the work is not a "text" to be read but rather a "fully multimedia work in which screen design and software functionality are part of its signifying practices."[11] While having some links to previous hypertext conventions, Memmott's work has clearly moved into another sphere of creative engagement that requires a host of new conventions and practices for creators, readers and critics.

While certainly intriguing, highly experimental works, such as those of Memmott, Amerika or JODI, are not the only indicators of hypertext's future. In fact, one may criticize Hayles for continuing the practice of using highly experimental works as the primary exemplars for theorizing the nature of electronic "texts." Such a move indicates the familiar bias toward "difficult" works, which is to say works that defy or work against normative conventions. This has a curious "modernist" tinge to it in a manner that parallels the aesthetic biases of both modernism and postmodernism in which the conventions of tradition and the status quo are consistently challenged or at least positioned as something to go beyond. In the case of hypertext, this bias is clearly indicated by the sustained emphasis on experimentation (in the tradition of experimental literature) and a discourse that positions hypertext as a revolutionary and evolutionary force. Hayles's celebratory treatment of works by Talan Memmott, Tom Phillips and Mark Z. Danielewski could be seen as continuing a discursive regime that I coin as (re)evolutionary. In other words, what is worthy of critical reflection and acknowledgment are works that explicitly push the conceptual and aesthetic envelopes in a manner that advances the medium, genre or discipline. Works or phenomena that appear "normal" are, in contrast, rarely given much thought.

Accordingly, the future of hypertext also lies in practices that are not exclusively situated in the rarified worlds of experimental art and literature nor in the types of aesthetic and conceptual contexts favored by critics and philosophers. Equally telling of the material complexities of the electronic text (to use Hayles's generic term) are the mundane, everyday phenomena such as blogs, Web diaries, SMS, handheld game devices and Apple Computer's new "Tiger" operating system. Each in its own way reveals a host of tantalizing issues about the nature of interaction, the relationship between creators and audiences and the materialities of interfaces, content and users in an increasingly mobile communications environment. Consider, for example, the "Spotlight" feature in Tiger. Described as a "constantly updated index that sees all the metadata inside supported files," Spotlight offers an apparently intuitive search engine that allows me to locate, organize and contextualize the content of my increasingly crowded hard drive.[12] What is notable about the Spotlight agent is that it augments my very much diminished ability to keep track of and locate the content of my computer system. While I would not exactly term my Powerbook as an "intimate supplement to my memory," it does contain a great deal of what constitutes my identity and role as a professional academic. That I am increasingly reliant on a search engine to access this content reveals something about the manner in which this technology has impacted the material condition of my life, especially my professional and creative life.

Likewise, the phenomena of online diary writing and Web cams, as I have explored in much more detail elsewhere, provide a compelling example of how the representation of self via the written word has been transformed by the specific characteristics of the World Wide Web and the material conditions of the network society.[13] Especially relevant to the discussion of hypertext is the Web's ability to transform itself by virtue of reader input that, in turn, transforms the reader's interaction with and agency within the World Wide Web. This relentless feedback loop takes on special significance in the case of Web-based "self-documentation," which is composed of a complex of connections between the internal world of personal experience and a defined but potentially limitless community or network of communicative readers. As in some literary hypertexts, a portion of the interpretive dynamics is based on the ability to and interest in maintaining an active link with actual and potential readers via a multilevel interplay that moves seamlessly between the subjective spaces of personal experience or reflection and the relatively distanced activity of exploring a text or Web site for reasons that range from genuine interest to distracted voyeurism. In this way, Web diaries become "living texts" in a manner that is similar to the dynamism of hypermedia in so much that they can potentially represent, to quote Ted Nelson, "the true content and structure of human thought."[14]

All of this is to argue that writing and expression in the digital age cannot be fully represented by only paying attention to what is created within an explicitly artistic or professional context. What we know and experience as hypertext also takes place in our everyday interactions with the technologies we use to express and represent ourselves to those around us. Equally pertinent is that the theoretical, aesthetic, political and formal concerns of hypertext have relevance and application beyond the immediate domain of hypertext as conceived and practiced by the normative hypertext community. This has largely to do with the fact that "writing" and the nature of "text" have been considerably augmented, stretched and "complexified" within the context of global information technology and the material specificities of its economic, technical, political, aesthetic and cultural infrastructures. Thus, the fate of the reader and writer and the conditions and demands of the electronic text can be explored and developed within arenas and via interfaces that go far beyond what we know today as hypertext and hypermedia. And lastly, the answer to my question—what is the future of hypertext?—is as follows: The future of hypertext, is all around us. All we have to do is pay attention.

Notes

Introduction

1 Theodor Nelson, *Literary Machines 93.1* (Sausalito, CA: Mindful Press, 1992).
2 Mark Taylor and Esa Saarinen, *Imagologies: Media Philosophy* (London: Routledge, 1994), 6.
3 George Landow, *Hypertext: The Convergence of Contemporary Critical Theory and Technology* (Baltimore: Johns Hopkins University Press, 1992), 24.
4 Jody Berland, "Cultural Technologies and the Evolution of Technological Cultures." In *The World Wide Web and Contemporary Cultural Theory*. Ed. Andrew Herman and Thomas Swiss (New York: Routledge, 2000), 236.

1 A Brief History of Hypertext

1 Hayden White. "Foreword." Reinhart Koselleck, *The Practice of Conceptual History: Timing History, Spacing Concepts* (Stanford, CA: Stanford University Press, 2002), ix.
2 R. Alexander Galloway, *Protocol: How Control Exists After Decentralization* (Cambridge, MA: MIT Press, 2004), xii.
3 J. David Bolter, *Writing Space: Computers, Hypertext, and the Remediation of Print* (Mahwah, NJ: Lawrence Erlbaum, 2001), 15.
4 N. Katherine Hayles, *Writing Machines* (Cambridge, MA: MIT Press, 2002), 19.
5 Walter Ong, *Orality and Literacy: The Technologizing of the Word* (New York: Routledge, 2002).
6 J. David Bolter, *Writing Space: The Computer, Hypertext, and the History of Writing* (Hillsdale, NJ: Lawrence Erlbaum, 1991), 59.
7 Harold A. Innis, *The Bias of Communication* (Toronto: University of Toronto Press, 1951).
8 Robert Coover, "The End of Books." *New York Times Book Review*, June 21, 1992, sec. 1, 23–25.
9 Bolter, *Writing Space: Computers*, xii.
10 J. Yellowlees Douglas, *The End of Books or Books Without End?: Reading Interactive Narratives* (Ann Arbor: University of Michigan Press, 2000), 3.
11 The sections on Bush and Nelson are taken from my article "Pioneer Spirits and the Lure of Technology: Vannevar Bush's Desk, Theodor Nelson's World." *Configurations*, 2001, 9, 441–459.
12 Vannevar Bush, "As We May Think." *Atlantic Monthly*, July 1945, 101–108.

13 The memex is described on pp. 107 and 108 of Bush, "As We May Think."
14 Ibid., 106.
15 Vannevar Bush, "Memex II." In *From Memex to Hypertext: Vannevar Bush and the Mind's Machine*. Ed. James Nyce and Paul Kahn (New York: Academic Press, 1991), 167.
16 Nelson's texts are full of such claims. See, for instance, p. 58 of *Computer Lib/Dream Machines*. Self-published, 1974, or browse at random through *The Home Computer Revolution*, self-published, 1977.
17 Theodor Nelson. *Literary Machines 93.1. Sausalito, Calif: Mindful Press*, 1992, p. "1/20."
18 Theodor Nelson, "Opening Hypertext: A Memoir." In *Literacy Online: The Promise and Peril of Reading and Writing with Computers*. Ed. Myron Tuman (Pittsburgh: University of Pittsburgh, 1992), 45–48.
19 Nelson, *Computer Lib*, p. DM44 (DM refers to the *Dream Machine* portion of the publication).
20 Ibid., p. DM19.
21 Ibid., p. DM45.
22 This is Nelson's "real dream" mentioned earlier.
23 Douglas Engelbart, "The Augmented Knowledge Workshop." In *A History of Personal Workstations*. Ed. Adele Goldberg (New York: ACM Press, 1988), 188–189.
24 Streaming QuickTime footage of the entire demo is available at "Doug Engelbart 1968 Demo." <http://sloan.stanford.edu/MouseSite/1968Demo.html> (September 14, 2005).
25 N. Yankelovich, B.J. Haan and S.M. Drucker, "Connections in Context." *Proceedings of the Twenty-First Annual Hawaii International Conference on Software Track* (Los Alamitos, CA: IEEE Computer Society Press, 1988), 715.
26 The Victorian Web. <http://www.scholars.nus.edu.sg/landow/victorian/> (September 14, 2005).
27 For detailed information about the Victorian Web, see Landow's *Hypertext 2.0. The Convergence of Contemporary Critical Theory and Technology* (Baltimore: Johns Hopkins University Press, 1997).
28 International HyperCard User Group. <http://www.ihug.org/> (September 14, 2005).
29 N. Yankelovich, B.J. Haan, N.K. Meyrowitz and S.M. Drucker, "Intermedia: The Concept and the Construction of a Seamless Information Environment." *IEEE Computer*, January 1988, 81–96.
30 P.J. Nürnberg, J.J. Leggett and E.R. Schneider, "As We Should Have Thought." *Proceedings of the Eighth ACM Conference on Hypertext* (Southampton, UK: ACM Press, 1997), 97.
31 Mark Bernstein, "Storyspace 1." *Proceedings of the 13th ACM Conference on Hypertext and Hypermedia 2002* (Maryland: ACM, 2002), 172–181.
32 Carolyn Guyer, *Quibbling* (Watertown, MA: Eastgate Systems, 1992).
33 For additional titles, see "The Eastgate Systems Catalog." ca. 2005 <http://www.eastgate.com/storyspace/> (September 14, 2005).
34 Michael Joyce, "Storyspace as a Hypertext System for Writers and Readers of Varying Ability." *Proceedings of the Third Annual ACM Conference on Hypertext* (New York: ACM Press, 1991), 383–384.
35 "Praise for Storyspace" in "Storyspace Overview." <http://www.eastgate.com/storyspace/> (September 14, 2005).
36 Voyager's complete catalog can be seen at <http://www.bringyourbrain.com/.> (September 14, 2005).
37 Sean Silverthorne, "Paperless Writer: The Voyager Co's CD ROM Publishing Adventures." *PC Week Inside*, July 17, 1995, 12(28), A5(1).
38 Ibid.
39 "The Radical" in "The Edge." <http://www.edge.org/digerati/stein/> (October 25, 2005).

40 Minne Buwalda, "Voyager." *Mediamatic*. Special vol. 7(3/4). End of advertising issue http://www.mediamatic.net/article–200.5847.html
41 Jim Ottaviani, "Expanded Book Toolkit (Software Review)." *Library Software Review*, Winter 1993, 12(4), 74–75.
42 After the demise of Voyager, Bob Stein created "Night Kitchen," which was intended to provide multimedia tools for a mass audience and "change the future of desktop publishing." Though the company's Web site is still online, it has not been updated since 2001 and there are no current reports or commentary about the company in the press. See <http://www.nightkitchen.com> for more details.
43 HT: Conference on Hypertext and Hypermedia. "Description." ACM *Portal Consortia*, ca. 2005 <http://portal.acm.org> (September 14, 2005).
44 Galloway, *Protocol*, 29.
45 Howard Rheingold is a pioneer in pursuing and exploring the social and cultural impact of the Internet and other information technologies. See his classic *The Virtual Community: Homesteading on the Electronic Frontier* (Reading, MA: Addison–Wesley Publishing Co., 1993).
46 Tim Berners-Lee, "The World Wide Web: A Very Short Personal History." *WC3: World Wide Web Consortium*. Date unknown. <http://www.w3.org/People/Berners–Lee/ShortHistory> (September 14, 2005).
47 Andrew Feenberg, *Critical Theory of Technology* (Oxford: Oxford University Press, 1991), 78.
48 Ibid., 80.
49 Ibid., 81.
50 Jody Berland, "Cultural Technologies and the Evolution of Technological Cultures." In *The World Wide Web and Contemporary Cultural Theory*. Ed. Andrew Herman and Thomas Swiss (New York: Routledge, 2000), 242.
51 Vivian Sobchack, "The Scene of the Screen: Envisioning Cinematic and Electronic Presence." In *Electronic Media and Technoculture*. Ed. John T. Caldwell (New Brunswick, NJ: Rutgers University Press, 2000), 138.
52 Mark Amerika, "Expanding the Concept of Writing: Notes on Net Art, Digital Narrative and Viral Ethics." *Leonardo*, 2004, 37(1), 12.

2 Hypertext Use

1 J. Yellowlees Douglas, *The End of Books or Books Without End?: Reading Interactive Narratives* (Ann Arbor: University of Michigan Press, 2000), 8.
2 Robert Coover, "Literary Hypertext: The Passing of the Golden Age." Keynote Address, Digital Arts and Culture, Atlanta, Georgia, October 29, 1999. <http://nickm.com/vox/golden_age.html> (September 14, 2005).
3 Judy Malloy, "Preface: Revelations of Secret Surveillance." ca. 2004. <http://www.well.com/user/jmalloy/gunterandgwen/aboutrevss.html> (September 14, 2005).
4 Judy Malloy, "From Narrabase of Hyperfiction: Uncle Roger." ca. 1991. <http://www.well.com/user/jmalloy/rogpap.html> (September 14, 2005).
5 Judy Malloy, "Preface." <http://www.well.com/user/jmalloy/gunterandgwen/ notesgg.html> (September 14, 2005).
6 Linda Carroli and Josephine Wilson, "Water Writes Always in Plural." March 1998. <http://ensemble.va.com.au/water/index.html> (September 14, 2005).
7 Mark Amerika, "Expanding the Concept of Writing: Notes on Net Art, Digital Narrative and Viral Ethics." *Leonardo*, 2004, 37:1, 9.

8 Mark Amerika, *Filmtext 2.0.* ca. 2002 <http://www.markamerika.com/filmtext/> (September 14, 2005).
9 Amerika, "Expanding the Concept of Writing," 9.
10 Carl Franklin and Susan Kinnel, *Hypertext/Hypermedia in Schools—A Resource Book.* (Santa Barbara, CA: ABC-CLIO, 1990), xv.
11 Theodor Nelson, "Computer Lib/Dream Machines." In *The New Media Reader*. Ed. Noah Wardrip-Fruin and Nick Montfort (Cambridge, MA: The MIT Press, 2003), 312.
12 George Landow, *Hypertext 2.0: The Convergence of Contemporary Literary Theory and Technology* (Baltimore: Johns Hopkins University Press, 1997), 220.
13 Japie Heydenrych, "Avoiding a Tired and Stale Pedagogy: Activating On-Line Learning" *Progressio*, 2001, 23:2. <http://www.unisa.ac.za/default.asp?Cmd=ViewContent&ContentID=13269> (September 14, 2005).
14 "Net Frog: The On-Line Dissection." November 7, 2002. <http://curry.edschool.virginia.edu/go/frog/Frog2/> (September 14, 2005).
15 M.S. Bauer, N. Glickman, L. Glickman, J.P. Toombs and P. Bill. "Evaluation of the Effectiveness of a Cadaver Laboratory during a Fourth-Year Veterinary Surgery Rotation." *Journal of Veterinary Medical Education*, 1992, 19:2, 77–84. See also P.S. Cohen and M. Block, "Replacement of Laboratory Animals in an Introductory Psychology Laboratory." *Humane Innovations and Alternatives*, 1991, 5, 221–225.
16 Landow, *Hypertext 2.0*, 241.
17 Ibid., 236.
18 Ibid., 223.
19 Wendi Maloney, "Brick and Mortar Campuses Go Online." *Academe Online*, September–October 1999, 85:9.
20 http://xanadu.com/
21 Landow, *Hypertext 2.0*, 265.
22 Lars Hubrich, "HyperX: An Interview with George Landow." Date Unknown. <http://www.altx.com/int2/george.landow.html> (September 14, 2005).
23 Mark Bernstein, "Patterns of Hypertext." ca. 1998. <http://www.eastgate.com/patterns/Print.html> (September 14, 2005).
24 Hal Berghel, "The Inevitable Demise of the Web." *ACM SIGAPP Applied Computing Review*, Fall 1995, 3:2, 5.
25 Ibid., 6.
26 Jonathan Grudin. "Computer-Supported Cooperative Work: History and Focus. *Computer*, May 1994, 19–26.
27 Ibid., 21.
28 Norbert Streltz, Frank Halasz, Hiroshi Ishii, Tom Malone, Chris Neuwirth and Gary Olson, "The Role of Hypertext for CSCW Applications." *Proceedings of the Third Annual ACM Conference on Hypertext*, September 1991, 369.
29 Ibid., 372.
30 Jörg Haake and Weigang Wang, "Flexible Support for Business Processes: Extending Cooperative Hypermedia with Process Support." *Information and Software Technology*, 1999, 41, 358.
31 Richard Hull and Roger King. "Semantic Database Modelling: Survey, Applications, and Research Issues." *ACM Computing Surveys*, September 1987, 19:3, 201.
32 Haake and Wang, "Flexible Support," 359.
33 Timothy Miles-Board and Leslie Carr. "Supporting Management Reporting: A Writable Web Case Study." *Conference Proceedings. WWW2003*, May 20–24, 2003, Budapest, Hungary.

34 Ibid., 238.

35 Espen Aarseth, "Computer Game Studies, Year One. Game Studies." *The International Journal of Computer Game Research*, 2001, 1:1. <http://gamestudies.org/0101/editorial.html> (September 15, 2005).

36 Markku Eskelinen, "Towards Computer Game Studies." In *First Person. New Media as Story, Performance, and Game*. Ed. Pat Harrigan and Noah Wardrip-Fruin (Cambridge, MA: MIT Press, 2003), 36.

37 Gonzalo Frasca, "Simulation versus Narrative: Introduction to Ludology." In *The Video Game Reader*. Ed. Mark J.P. Wolf and Bernard Perron (New York: Routledge, 2003), 222.

38 Katherine Hayles, "Print is Flat, Code is Deep: The Importance of Media-Specific Analysis." *Poetics Today*, Spring 2004, 25, 67.

39 Geoffrey Rockwell, "Gore Galore: Literary Theory and Computer Games." *Computers and the Humanities*, 2002, 36:3, 348.

40 Nick Montfort, *Twisty Little Passages: An Approach to Interactive Fiction* (Cambridge, MA: MIT Press, 2003), 9.

41 Sarah Sloane, *Digital Fictions: Storytelling in a Material World* (Westport, CT: Ablex Publishing, 2000), 82.

42 Ibid., 83.

43 Mark Blanc, *Deadline*. Infocom, 1982. See <http://www.infocom-if.org/games/deadline/dealine.html> for a brief description.

44 Sloane, *Digital Fictions*, 84.

45 Dennis Jerz. "Colossal Cave Adventure—Will Crowther (c1975): Will Crowther and Don Woods (1976)" <http://jerz.setonhill.edu/if/canon/Adventure.htm> (September 14, 2005).

46 The original version of Adventure written by Crowther is no longer available but numerous versions of the Crowther and Woods remake are available on the World Wide Web. As with many things on the Web, it is difficult to assess the reliability of these versions in terms of their being what they say they are. One of the more comprehensive sites for accessing past and present works of interactive fiction is the "Interactive Fiction Archive" available at http://www.ifarchive.org. On this site you can find Crowther and Woods's original FORTRAN source code written for the PDP-10 computer along with various other versions that will run on contemporary machines. Another reliable version of Adventure, one would hope, can be found on the CD-ROM that accompanies MIT's *New Media Reader*, edited by Noah Wardrip-Fruin and Nick Montfort.

47 Janet Murray, *Hamlet on the Holodeck: The Future of Narrative in Cyberspace* (Cambridge, MA: MIT Press, 1997), 98–99.

48 See, for example, Ralph Lombreglia's review of Riven for *The Atlantic*. "Digital Culture," 98.01.

49 Alison McMahan, "Immersion, Engagement, and Presence." In Wolf and Perron, 68–69.

50 Emily Brown and Paul Cairns, "Grounded Investigation of Game Immersion." *CHI 2004*, Late Breaking Results Paper, April 24–29, 2004, Vienna, Austria, p. 1300.

51 Michael Joyce, "Siren Shapes: Exploratory and Constructive Hypertexts." *Academic Computing*, November 1988, 11.

52 Douglas, "*The Pleasures of Immersion and Engagement: schemas, scripts and the fifth business*." Digital Creativity. *Volume 12, Number 3, Sept. 2001, 163*.

53 Ibid., 161.

54 Brown and Cairns, "Grounded Investigation," 1299.

55 This claim will be pursued in more detail in the next chapter.

56 Natalie Bookchin, "The Intruder." ca. 1999. <http://www.calarts.edu/~bookchin/intruder/> (September 14, 2005).

57 Bookchin, "The Intruder." In *Frontiers: A Journal of Women Studies*, 2005, 26:1, 43–47.

58 Espen Aarseth, *Cybertext: Perspectives on Ergodic Literature* (Baltimore: Johns Hopkins University Press, 1997), 1.

59 Gonzalo Frasca. "Simulation versus Narrative," In Wolf and Perron, 233.

60 Stuart Moulthrop, "Hegirascope." Version 2. October 1997. <http://iat.ubalt.edu/moulthrop/hypertexts/hgs/> (September 15, 2005).

61 A comparable and far more recent approach was taken by Young-Hae Chang Heavy Industries in "The Last Days of Betty Nkomo." *Poems That Go*. Winter 2004, no. 15. <http://www.poemsthatgo.com/poems.htm> (September 15, 2005).

62 Juul's model is composed of the following elements:

   1 Game state: The state of the game at a given time.
   2 Play time: The time used by the player to play the game.
   3 Event time: The time of the events in the game.
   4 Mapping: The process of claiming that what the player does is also something in event time; projection of the play time onto event time.
   5 Speed: The relation between the play time and the event time.
   6 Fixation: The historical time of the event time, if any.
   7 Cut-scenes: When the event time is constructed through narration (i.e., told rather than played).

   Jesper Juul, "Introduction to Game Time." In Wardrip-Fruin and Harrigan, 131–142.

63 "Text Rain" in "Projects." Camille Utterback. ca. 1999. <http://www.camilleutterback.com/textrain.html> September 14, 2005.

64 Jay Bolter and Diane Gromala, *Windows and Mirrors: Interaction Design, Digital Art, and the Myth of Transparency* (Cambridge, MA: MIT Press, 2003), 25.

65 Ibid., 25.

66 Eric Zimmerman, "Narrative, Interactivity, Play and Games." In Wardrip-Fruin and Harrigan, 159.

67 Jim Miller, "Storytelling Evolves on the Web: Case Study: EXOCOG and the Future of Storytelling." *Interactions*, 2005, 12:1, 3.

68 Barry Atkins, *More Than a Game: The Computer Game as Fictional Form* (Manchester: Manchester University Press, 2003), 154.

3 Theorization of Hypertext

1 Marie-Laure Ryan, "Beyond Myth and Metaphor: The Case of Narrative in Digital Media." *Game Studies: The International Journal of Computer Game Research*. Volume 1, issue no. 1, July 2001. <http://www.gamestudies.org> (September 14, 2005).

2 George Landow, *Hypertext 2.0. The Convergence of Contemporary Critical Theory and Technology* (Baltimore: Johns Hopkins University Press, 1997), 2.

3 Ibid., 2.

4 Sherry Turkle, *Life on the Screen: Identity in the Age of the Internet* (New York: Simon & Schuster, 1997).

5 See, for example, Lev Manovich's introduction to the *New Media Reader*. "New Media from Borges to HTML." In *The New Media Reader*. Ed. Noah Wardrip-Fruin and Nick Montfort (Cambridge, MA: MIT Press, 2003), 13–25.

6 As quoted in Landow, *Hypertext 2.0*, 3.

7 Ibid., 33.

8 J. Yellowlees Douglas, *The End of Books: Or Books Without End?: Reading Interactive Narratives* (Ann Arbor: University of Michigan Press: 2000), 133–134.
9 Katherine Hayles, "Print is Flat, Code is Deep: The Importance of Media Specific Analysis." *Poetics Today*, Spring 2004, 25:1, 77.
10 Ibid., 81.
11 Landow, *Hypertext 2.0*, 10.
12 L.M. Dryden, "Literature, Student-Centered Classrooms, and Hypermedia Environments." In *Literacy and Computers: The Complications of Teaching and Learning with Technology*. Ed. C.L. Selfe and S. Hilligoss (New York: Modern Language Association, 1994), 285.
13 Davida Charney, "The Impact of Hypertext on Processes of Reading and Writing." In Hilligoss and Selfe, 238–262.
14 Landow, *Hypertext 2.0*, 275. There is a rich tradition of scholarship that deals with such issues. Among the more familiar are the ideas of Harold Innis, Marshall McLuhan and Martin Heidegger.
15 David Bolter, "Degrees of Freedom." 1995. <http://www.lcc.gatech.edu/bolter/degrees.html> September 14, 2005).
16 Roland Barthes, *Image/Music/Text* (New York: Hill & Wang, 1977), 142.
17 Ibid., 142.
18 Ilana Snyder, *Hypertext: The Electronic Labyrinth* (New York: New York University Press, 1996), 62.
19 Landow, *Hypertext 2.0*, 5.
20 Henning Ziegler, "Why Hypertext Became Uncool: Notes on Power, Politics and the Interface." *Dichtung-Digital: Contributions on Digital Aesthetics*. Issue 1 (2003). <http://www.dichtung-digital.org/2003/issue/1/ziegler/> (September 14, 2005).
21 Marie-Laure Ryan, "Beyond Myth and Metaphor: The Case of Narrative in Digital Media." *Game Studies*, 2001, 1:1. <http://www.gamestudies.org> (September 15, 2005).
22 Espen Aarseth, *Cybertext: Perspectives on Ergodic Literature* (Baltimore: Johns Hopkins University Press, 1997), 3.
23 Nick Montfort, "Cybertext Killed the Hypertext Star." "Threads Reviews" *ebr* 11 "Web Arts" 00/01 (2001). <http://www.altx.com/ebr/ebr11/11mon/index.html> (September 14, 2005).
24 Aarseth, *Cybertext*, 4.
25 Ibid., 22.
26 Ibid., 14.
27 Jean François Lyotard, *The Postmodern Condition: A Report on Knowledge*. Trans. Geoff Bennington and Brian Massumi (Minneapolis: University of Minnesota Press, 1984).
28 Douglas Kellner, *Media Culture: Cultural Studies, Identity and Politics between the Modern and the Postmodern* (New York: Routledge, 1995).
29 Rob Witting, *Invisible Rendezvous: Connection and Collaboration in the New Landscape of Electronic Writing* (Middletown, CT: Wesleyan University Press, 1994), 8.
30 Fredric Jameson, *Postmodernism: Or the Cultural Logic of Late Capitalism* (Durham, NC: Duke University Press, 1997).
31 See, for example, Mark Poster, *The Mode of Information: Poststructuralism and Social Context* (Chicago: University of Chicago Press, 1990).
32 Stuart Moulthrop, "Hypertext and the Hyperreal." *Hypertext 89 Proceedings*. November 1989, 259.
33 David Harvey, *The Condition of Post Modernity: An Enquiry Into the Origins of Cultural Change* (Oxford: Blackwell, 1989).

34 Johndan Johnson-Eilola, *Nostalgic Angels: Rearticulating Hypertext Writing* (New Jersey: Ablex Publishing Company, 1997), 132.
35 Manuel Castells, *The Information Age: Economy, Society and Culture*, vol. 1 (Oxford: Blackwell, 1998), 3.
36 Andrew Feenberg, *Critical Theory of Technology* (Oxford: Oxford University Press, 1991), 14.
37 The last few pages of this chapter are drawn from my article "Parables of the Network: The Lures and Spoils of Global Economics." *Convergence: The Journal of Research into New Media Technologies*, Autumn 1998, 3:3.
38 Castells, *The Information Age*, 4.
39 Mark Poster, *The Second Media Age* (Cambridge: Polity Press, 1995), 57.
40 Wendy Morgan, "Hypertext 1999 Proceedings." ACM 1999, 210.
41 Arthur Kroker, "Virtual Capitalism." In *Techno-Science and Cyber Culture*. Ed. Stanley Aronowitz (New York: Routledge, 1996), 168.
42 Michael Joyce, *Othermindedness: The Emergence of Network Culture* (Ann Arbor: University of Michigan Press, 2000), 3.

4 The Future of Hypertext

1 Robert Coover, "Literary Hypertext: The Passing of the Golden Age." October 29, 1999. Keynote Address, Digital Arts and Culture, Atlanta, Georgia. <http://www.nickm.com/vox/golden_age.html> (September 14, 2005).
2 Ibid.
3 Ibid.
4 Mark Hansen. *Embodying Technesis: Technology Beyond Writing* (Ann Arbor: University of Michigan Press, 2000), 234.
5 Ibid., 3.
6 Part of this passage is based on a similar argument pursued in my book *Saved From Oblivion: Documenting the Daily from Diaries to Web Cams* (New York: Peter Lang, 2004), 4–5, 36.
7 Katherine Hayles. *Writing Machines* (Cambridge, Mass.: MIT Press, 2002), 42.
8 Ibid., 41.
9 Ibid, 25.
10 Talan Memmott, "Lexia to Perplexia." ca. 2000. <http://www.uiowa.edu/~iareview/tirweb/hypermedia/talan_memmott/> (September 14, 2005).
11 Hayles, 56.
12 Spotlight. Apple Computer. <http://www.apple.com/macosx/features/spotlight/> (September 14, 2005).
13 Andreas Kitzmann, *Saved From Oblivion*. Also "That Different Place: Documenting the Self Within On-Line Environments." *Biography: An Interdisciplinary Quarterly*, Winter 2003, 26:1.
14 Theodor Nelson, "Computer Lib/Dream Machines." In *The New Media Reader*, Ed. Noah Wardrip–Fruin and Nick Montfort (Cambridge, MA: The MIT Press, 2003), 326.

Bibliography

Aarseth, Espen. *Cybertext: Perspectives on Ergodic Literature*. Baltimore: John Hopkins University Press, 1997.

Aarseth, Espen. "Computer Game Studies, Year One. Game Studies." *The International Journal of Computer Game Research*, 1:1 (2001). http://gamestudies.org/0101/editorial.html, Last accessed on September 15, 2005.

Amerika, Mark. "Expanding the Concept of Writing: Notes on Net Art, Digital Narrative and Viral Ethics." *Leonardo*, 37:1 (2004), 9.

Amerika, Mark. "*Filmtext* 2.0." ca. 2002 http://www.markamerika.com/*filmtext*/, Last accessed on September 14, 2005.

Atkins, Barry. *More Than a Game: The Computer Game as Fictional Form*. Manchester: Manchester University Press, 2003.

Barthes, Roland. *Image/Music/Text*. New York: Hill & Wang, 1977.

Bauer, M.S., N. Glickman, L. Glickman, J.P. Toombs and P. Bill. "Evaluation of the Effectiveness of a Cadaver Laboratory During a Fourth-Year Veterinary Surgery Rotation." *Journal of Veterinary Medical Education* 19:2 (1992), 77–84.

Berghel, Hal. "The Inevitable Demise of the Web." *ACM SIGAPP Applied Computing Review*, 3:2 (Fall 1995), 5.

Berland, Jody. "Cultural Technologies and the Evolution of Technological Cultures." In *The World Wide Web and Contemporary Cultural Theory*. Ed. Andrew Herman and Thomas Swiss. New York: Routledge, 2000.

Bernstein, Mark. "Patterns of Hypertext." ca. 1998. http://www.eastgate.com/patterns/Print.html, Last accessed on September 14, 2005.

Bernstein, Mark. "Storyspace 1." *Proceedings of the 13th ACM Conference on Hypertext and Hypermedia 2002*. Maryland: ACM, 2002.

Blanc, Mark. *Deadline*. Infocom, 1982. http://www.infocom-if.org/games/deadline/deadline.html, Last accessed on September 14, 2005.

Bolter, Jay, D. *Writing Space: The Computer, Hypertext, and the History of Writing*. Hillsdale, NJ: Lawrence Erlbaum, 1991.

Bolter, David. "Degrees of Freedom." 1995. http://www.lcc.gatech.edu/-bolter/degrees.html, Last accessed on September 4, 2005.

Bolter, David, J. *Writing Space: Computers, Hypertext, and the Remediation of Print*. Mahwah, NJ: Lawrence Erlbaum, 2001.

Bolter, Jay and Diane Gromala. *Windows and Mirrors: Interaction Design, Digital Art, and the Myth of Transparency*. Cambridge, MA: MIT Press, 2003.

Bookchin, Natalie. "The Intruder." ca. 1999. http://www.calarts.edu/~bookchin/intruder/, Last accessed on September 14, 2005.

Bookchin, Natalie. "The Intruder." *Frontiers: A Journal of Women Studies*, 26:1 (2005), 43–47.

Brown, Emily and Paul Cairns. "Grounded Investigation of Game Immersion." *CHI 2004* Late Breaking Results Paper, April 24–29, 2004, Vienna, Austria, p. 1300.

Bush, Vannevar. "As We May Think." *Atlantic Monthly* (July 1945), 101–108.

Bush, Vannevar. "Memex II." In *From Memex to Hypertext: Vannevar Bush and the Mind's Machine*. Ed. James Nyce and Paul Kahn. New York: Academic Press, 1991.

Carroli, Linda and Josephine Wilson,. "Water Writes Always in Plural." March 1998. http://ensemble.va.com.au/water/index.html, Last accessed on September 14, 2005.

Castells, Manuel. *The Information Age: Economy, Society and Culture*, vol. 1. Oxford: Blackwell, 1998.

Chang, Young-Hae. "The Last Days of Betty Nkomo." *Poems That Go* (Winter 2004, Number 15). http://www.poemsthatgo.com/

Charney, Davida. "The Impact of Hypertext on Processes of Reading and Writing." In *Literacy and Computers*. Ed. S. Hilligoss and C. Selfe. New York: Modern Language Association, 1993.

Cohen, P.S. and M. Block. "Replacement of Laboratory Animals in an Introductory Psychology Laboratory." *Humane Innovations and Alternatives*, 5 (1991), 221–225.

Coover, Robert. "The End of Books." *New York Times Book Review* (June 21, 1992), sec 1, 23–25.

Coover, Robert. "Literary Hypertext: The Passing of the Golden Age." Keynote Address, Digital Arts and Culture, Atlanta, Georgia, October 29, 1999. http://www.nickm.com/vox/golden_age.html, Last accessed on September 14, 2005.

Douglas, J. Yellowlees. *The End of Books or Books Without End?: Reading Interactive Narratives*. Ann Arbor: University of Michigan Press, 2000.

Dryden, L.M. "Literature, Student-Centered Classrooms, and Hypermedia Environments." In *Literacy and Computers: The Complications of Teaching and Learning with Technology*. Ed. C.L. Selfe and S. Hilligoss. New York: Modern Language Association, 1994.

"The Eastgate Systems Catalog." ca. 2005. http://www.eastgate.com/storyspace/, Last accessed on September 14, 2005.

Engelbart, Douglas. "The Augmented Knowledge Workshop." In *A History of Personal Workstations*. Ed. Adele Goldberg. New York: ACM Press, 1988.

Eskelinen, Markku. "Towards Computer Game Studies." In *First Person. New Media as Story, Performance, and Game*. Ed. Noah Wardrip-Fruin and Pat Harrigan. Cambridge, MA: MIT Press, 2003.

Feenberg, Andrew. *Critical Theory of Technology*. Oxford: Oxford University Press, 1991.

Franklin, Carl and Susan Kinnel. *Hypertext/Hypermedia in Schools—A Resource Book*. Santa Barbara, CA: ABC-CLIO, 1990.

Frasca, Gonzalo. "Simulation versus Narrative: Introduction to Ludology." In *The Video Game Reader*. Ed. Mark J.P Wolf and Bernard Perron. New York: Routledge, 2003.

Galloway, Alexander, R. *Protocol: How Control Exists After Decentralization*. Cambridge, MA: MIT Press, 2004.

Grudin, Jonathan. "Computer-Supported Cooperative Work: History and Focus. *Computer* (May 1994), 19–26.

Guyer, Carolyn. *Quibbling*. Watertown, MA: Eastgate Systems, 1992.

Haake, Jorg. and Weigang Wang. "Flexible Support for Business Processes: Extending Cooperative Hypermedia with Process Support." *Information and Software Technology*, 41 (1999).

Hansen, Mark. *Embodying Technesis: Technology Beyond Writing*. Ann Arbor: University of Michigan Press, 2000.

Harvey, David. *The Condition of Post Modernity: An Enquiry Into the Origins of Cultural Change*. Oxford: Blackwell, 1989.

Hayles, Katherine, N. *Writing Machines*. Cambridge, MA: MIT Press, 2002.

Hayles, Katherine. "Print is Flat, Code is Deep: The Importance of Media-Specific Analysis." *Poetics Today*, 25:1 (Spring 2004), 67.

Heydenrych, Japie. "Avoiding a Tired and Stale Pedagogy: Activating On-line Learning." *Progressio*, 23:2 (2001). http://www.unisa.ac.za/default.asp?Cmd=ViewContent&ContentID=13269, Last accessed on September 14, 2005.

HT: Conference on Hypertext and Hypermedia. "Description". ACM Portal Consortia. ca. 2005. http://portal.acm.org, Last accessed on September 14, 2005.

Hubrich, Lars. "HyperX: An Interview with George Landow." Date Unknown. http://www.altx.com/int2/george.landow.html, Last accessed on September 14, 2005.

Hull, Richard and Roger King. "Semantic Database Modelling: Survey, Applications, and Research Issues." *ACM Computing Surveys*, 19:3 (September 1987).

Innis, Harold A. *The Bias of Communication*. Toronto: University of Toronto Press, 1951.

International HyperCard User Group. http://www.ihug.org/, Last accessed on September 4, 2005.

Jameson, Fredric. *Postmodernism: Or the Cultural Logic of Late Capitalism*. Durham, NC: Duke University Press, 1997.

Jerz, Dennis. "Colossal Cave Adventure—Will Crowther (c1975): Will Crowther and Don Woods (1976)." http://jerz.setonhill.edu/if/canon/Adventure.htm, Last accessed on September 14, 2005.

Johnson-Eilola, Johndan. *Nostalgic Angels: Rearticulating Hypertext Writing*. New Jersey: Ablex Publishing Company, 1997.

Joyce, Michael. "Siren Shapes: Exploratory and Constructive Hypertexts." *Academic Computing* (November 1988), 11

Joyce, Michael. "Storyspace as a Hypertext System for Writers and Readers of Varying Ability." *Proceedings of the Third Annual ACM Conference on Hypertext*. New York: ACM Press, 1991.

Joyce, Michael. *Othermindedness: The Emergence of Network Culture*. Ann Arbor: University of Michigan Press, 2000.

Kellner, Douglas. *Media Culture: Cultural Studies, Identity and Politics between the Modern and the Postmodern*. New York: Routledge, 1995.

Kitzmann, Andreas. "Parables of the Network: The Lures and Spoils of Global Economics." *Convergence: The Journal of Research into New Media Technologies*, 3:3 (Autumn 1998).

Kitzmann, Andreas. "Pioneer Spirits and the Lure of Technology: Vannevar Bush's Desk, Theodor Nelson's World." *Configurations*, 9 (2001), 441–459.

Kitzmann, Andreas. "That Different Place: Documenting the Self Within On-Line Environments." *Biography: An Interdisciplinary Quarterly*, 26:1 (Winter 2003).

Kitzmann, Andreas. *Saved from Oblivion: Documenting the Daily from Diaries to Web Cams*. New York: Peter Lang, 2004, pp. 4–5, 36.

Koselleck, Reinhart. *The Practice of Conceptual History: Timing History, Spacing Concepts*. Stanford, CA: Stanford University Press, 2002.

Kroker, Arthur. "Virtual Capitalism." In *Techno-Science and Cyber Culture*. Ed. Stanley Aronowitz. New York: Routledge, 1996.

Landow, George. *Hypertext: The Convergence of Contemporary Critical Theory and Technology*. Baltimore: John Hopkins University Press, 1992.

Landow, George. *Hypertext 2.0. The Convergence of Contemporary Critical Theory and Technology*. Baltimore: Johns Hopkins University Press, 1997.

Lee-Berners, Tim. "The World Wide Web: A Very Short Personal History." *WC3: World Wide Web Consortium*. Date Unknown. http://www.w3.org/People/Berners-Lee/ShortHistory, Last accessed on September 14, 2005.

Lyotard, Jean Francois. *The Postmodern Condition: A Report on Knowledge*. Trans. Geoff Bennington and Brian Massumi. Minneapolis: University of Minnesota Press, 1984.

Malloy, Judy. "From Narrabase of Hyperfiction: Uncle Roger." ca. 1991. http://www.well.com/user/jmalloy/rogpap.html, Last accessed on September 14, 2005.

Malloy, Judy. "Preface: Revelations of Secret Surveillance." ca. 2004. http://www.well.com/user/jmalloy/gunterandgwen/aboutrevss.html and http://www.well.com/user/jmalloy/gunterandgwen/notesgg.html, Last accessed on September 14, 2005.

Maloney, Wendi. "Brick and Mortar Campuses Go Online." *Academe Online*, 85:9 (September–October 1999).

Memmott, Talan. "Lexia to Perplexia." ca. 2000. http://www.uiowa.edu/~iareview/tirweb/hypermedia/talan_memmott/, September 14, 2005.

Miles-Board, Timothy and Leslie Carr. "Supporting Management Reporting: A Writable Web Case Study." *Conference Proceedings, WWW2003*, Budapest, Hungary (May 20–24, 2003).

Miller, Jim. "Storytelling Evolves on the Web: Case Study: EXOCOG and the Future of Storytelling." *Interactions*, 12:1 (2005).

Minne Buwalda. "Voyager." Mediamatic: Special vol. 7#3/4 End of Advertising Issue. http://www.mediamatic.net/article-200.5847.html.

Montfort, Nick. "Cybertext Killed the Hypertext Star." "Threads Reviews" *ebr* 11 "Web Arts" 11, 2001. http://www.altx.com/ebr/ebr11/11mon/index.html, Last accessed on September 14, 2005.

Montfort, Nick. *Twisty Little Passages: An Approach to Interactive Fiction*. Cambridge, MA: MIT Press, 2003.

Morgan, Wendy. "Hypertext 1999 Proceedings." ACM (1999), 210.

Moulthrop, Stuart. "Hypertext and the Hyperreal." *Hypertext 89 Proceedings* (November 1989).

Moulthrop, Stuart. "Hegirascope." Version 2. October 1997. http://iat.ubalt.edu/moulthrop/hypertexts/hgs/, Last accessed on September 15, 2005.

Murray, Janet. *Hamlet on the Holodeck: The Future of Narrative in Cyberspace*. Cambridge, MA: MIT Press, 1997.

Nelson, Theodor. *Computer Lib/Dream Machines*. Self-Published, 1974, p. DM44. (DM refers to the "Dream Machine" portion of the publication.)

Nelson, Theodor. "Opening Hypertext: A Memoir." *Literacy Online: The Promise and Peril of Reading and Writing with Computers*. Ed. Myron Tuman. Pittsburgh: University of Pittsburgh, 1992a.

Nelson, Theodor. *Literary Machines* 93.1. Sausalito, CA: Mindful Press, 1992b.

Nelson, Theodor. "Computer Lib/Dream Machines." In *The New Media Reader*. Ed. Noah Wardrip-Fruin and Nick Montfort. Cambridge, MA: The MIT Press, 2003.

Nelson, Theodor. "Xanadu." http://xanadu.com/, Last accessed on September 14, 2005.

"Net Frog: The On line Dissection." November 7, 2002. http://curry.edschool.virginia.edu/go/frog/Frog2/, Last accessed on September 14, 2005.

Nürnberg, P.J., J.J. Leggett and E.R. Schneider. "As We Should Have Thought." *Proceedings of the 8th ACM Conference on Hypertext*. Southampton, UK: ACM Press, 1997.

Ong, Walter. *Orality and Literacy: The Technologizing of the Word*. New York: Routledge, 2002.

Ottaviani, Jim. "Expanded Book Toolkit (Software Review)." *Library Software Review*, 12:4 (Winter 1993).

Poster, Mark. *The Mode of Information: Poststructuralism and Social Context*. Chicago: University of Chicago Press, 1990.

Poster, Mark. *The Second Media Age*. Cambridge, UK: Polity Press, 1995.

"Praise for Storyspace" in "Storyspace Overview." http://www.eastgate.com/storyspace/, Last accessed on September 14, 2005.

"The Radical" in "The Edge." http://www.edge.org/digerati/stein/, Last accessed on October 25, 2005.

Rheingold, Howard. *The Virtual Community: Homesteading on the Electronic Frontier*. Reading, MA: Addison-Wesley Pub. Co., 1993.

Rockwell, Geoffrey. "Gore Galore: Literary Theory and Computer Games." *Computers and the Humanities*, 36:3 (2002), 348.

Ryan, Marie-Laure. "Beyond Myth and Metaphor: The Case of Narrative in Digital Media." *Game Studies*, 1:1 (July 2001). http://www.gamestudies.org, Last accessed on September 15, 2005.

Silverthorne, Sean. "Paperless Writer: The Voyager Co's CD ROM Publishing Adventures." *PC Week Inside*, 12:28 (July 17, 1995), A5(1).

Sloane, Sarah. *Digital Fictions: Storytelling in a Material World*. Westport, CT: Ablex Publishing, 2000.

Snyder, Ilana. *Hypertext: The Electronic Labyrinth*. New York: New York University Press, 1996.

Sobchack, Vivian. "The Scene of the Screen: Envisioning Cinematic and Electronic Presence." In *Electronic Media and Technoculture*. Ed. John T. Caldwell. New Brunswick, NJ: Rutgers University Press, 2000.

Spotlight. Apple Computer. http://www.apple.com/macosx/features/spotlight/, Last accessed on September 14, 2005.

Streltz, Norbert, Frank Halasz, Hiroshi Ishii, Tom Malone, Chris Neuwirth and Gary Olson. "The Role of Hypertext for CSCW Applications." *Proceedings of the Third Annual ACM Conference on Hypertext* (September 1991).

Taylor, Mark and Esa Saarinen. *Imagologies: Media Philosophy*. London: Routledge, 1994.

Turkle, Sherry. *Life on the Screen: Identity in the Age of the Internet*. New York: Simon & Schuster, 1997.

Utterback, Camille. "Text Rain." In "Projects." ca. 1999. http://www.camilleutterback.com/textrain.html, Last accessed on September 14, 2005.

The Victorian Web. http://www.scholars.nus.edu.sg/landow/victorian/, Last accessed on September 4, 2005.

Wardrip-Fruin, Noah and Nick Montfort. Eds. *The New Media Reader*. Cambridge, MA: MIT Press, 2003.

Wardrip-Fruin, Noah and Pat Harrigan. Eds. *First Person: New Media as Story, Performance and Game*. Cambridge, MA: MIT Press, 2004.

Witting, Rob. *Invisible Rendezvous: Connection and Collaboration in the New Landscape of Electronic Writing*. Middletown, CT: Wesleyan University Press, 1994.

Yankelovich, N., B.J. Haan and S.M. Drucker. "Connections in Context." *Proceedings of the Twenty-First Annual Hawaii International Conference on Software Track*. Los Alamitos, CA: IEEE Computer Society Press (1988a).

Yankelovich, N., B.J. Haan, N.K. Meyrowitz and S.M. Drucker. "Intermedia: The Concept and the Construction of a Seamless Information Environment." *IEEE Computer* (January 1988b), 81–96.

Ziegler, Henning. "Why Hypertext Became Uncool: Notes on Power, Politics and the Interface." *Dichtung-Digital: Contributions on Digital Aesthetics*. 1 (2003). http://www.dichtung-digital.org/2003/issue/1/ziegler/, Last accessed on September 14, 2005.

Index